CK

D1288907

GRANT

THE SOLDIER

ULYSSES S. GRANT

Born, Point Pleasant, Ohio, April 27, 1822
Graduated, U. S. Military Academy, class of 1843
Served with distinction in Mexican War, 1846-1848
Married Julia Dent, St. Louis, Missouri, August 22, 1848
Resigned from the Army and returned to civil life, 1854
Commissioned as colonel, 21st Illinois Infantry, June 1861
Captured Fort Donelson by "Unconditional Surrender," Feb. 16, 1862
Decisive victory in the West, Vicksburg, July 4, 1863
Victory at Chattanooga, November 23-25, 1863
Promoted to command of the Union armies, March 2, 1864
Indecisive duel with Lee's army in Virginia, May-June, 1864
Besieged Petersburg, June 1864-April 1865
Received Lee's surrender at Appomattox, April 9, 1865
President of the United States, 1869-1877
Died at Mount McGregor, New York, July 23, 1885

GRANT THE SOLDIER

Edited by THOMAS M. PITKIN

Published by ACROPOLIS BOOKS

Colortone Building, Washington, D. C. 20009

in cooperation with the
Eastern National Park & Monument Association
© *Eastern National Park & Monument Association, 1965*

FIRST EDITION 1965

Library of Congress catalog card number 65-28302

This book was produced by Colortone Press, Washington, D. C. 20009

Type was photo composed on ATF Photo-typesetter and Intertype Fotosetter.
The text was set in ATF Caledonia, the subheads in Intertype Times Roman,
the captions in Intertype Century bold and italics.
The printing was done by lithography.

CONTENTS

vii

ILLUSTRATIONS

Note: *a single asterisk preceding an illustration title identifies the artist as Edwin Forbes; a double asterisk indicates Alfred R. Wanud. All are from wartime originals in the Collections of the Library of Congress.*

Cover: Gen. U.S. Grant *from a portrait by William Cogswell, 1867. Now displayed in the First Ladies' Hall, Smithsonian Institution, and reproduced with permission.*

INTRODUCTION

The overwhelming importance of the military decision reached at Appomattox in 1865 is unquestioned, but the proper place of General Ulysses S. Grant in American military annals is a matter of endless controversy. He has been praised without measure and blamed without restraint. During his military career and since he has been depicted both as a supreme genius worthy of comparison with Napoleon and as a blundering butcher who won his battles only through the reckless exploitation of superior numbers.

In our own time carefully documented and objective studies have appeared which will probably go a long way toward stilling the debate. Grant's failings have been fully set forth and his mistakes have been pointed out in detail, but his place as a great commander seems assured. At the same time, the high integrity and essential warmth of his personality become more apparent.

The present little volume does not attempt to add anything new in the way of interpretation. It does attempt to make a selection from the voluminous body of first-hand material that will bring Grant to life for the general reader.

In this book of sources Grant's own *Memoirs* have been freely drawn upon. For some phases of his early career they offer almost the only connected narrative available. For his part in the Civil War they present a clear, straight-forward account largely free from self-glorification and recrimination, an account that must be carefully considered in any full appraisal of the man. Though here and there the memory may be faulty, his essential spirit shines through the pages.

A good many of Grant's contemporaries have also been called upon to make their contributions. His relations with Lincoln, Sherman and Lee have been illustrated in their own words and in his. Lesser figures of that tremendous epoch in American history have been asked to throw light into dim corners of his career, or to show

Grant as he appeared to one and another who had a close view of him behind the growing and shifting facade of legend.

These selections have been arranged so as to form a narrative of Grant's life from his boyhood to the close of the Civil War, followed by illustration of his last days when his years in politics had been all but forgotten and he was living over again his life as a soldier. The editor has added only enough connective tissue to hold the body together.

It should be remembered, in reading these brief accounts by Grant and by men and women who knew him, that truth is a jewel of many facets; that all men are subject to error of observation; that memory falters; and that staff officers, like their commanders, are prone to exaggerate both the numbers and the losses of their opponents. But it is out of just such imperfect materials, supplied by fallible witnesses, that any historical fabric must be woven.

If this book helps to bring Ulysses S. Grant out of the mists of legend, and to make him appear a little more clearly as a man and a soldier, it will have served its purpose.

Thomas M. Pitkin
New York City

Boyhood on the Ohio

Grant wrote his Memoirs in final illness and in pain, but the work often gave him pleasure and the tone is generally cheerful and objective. There is little indication either of self-pity or of a tendency to romanticize in the recollections of his boyhood, quoted below. He was brought up in a community just emerging from frontier conditions and his father, Jesse Grant, was rapidly becoming a substantial business man. Life was hard, as seen from a modern perspective, but young Ulysses had most of the advantages that were available at the time and place.

I was born on the 27th of April, 1822, at Point Pleasant, Clermont County, Ohio. In the fall of 1823 we moved to Georgetown, the county seat of Brown, the adjoining county east. This place remained my home, until at the age of seventeen, in 1839, I went to West Point.

The schools, at the time of which I write, were very indifferent. There were no free schools, and none in which the scholars were classified. They were all supported by subscription, and a single teacher—who was often a man or a woman incapable of teaching much, even if they imparted all they knew—would have thirty or forty scholars, male and female, from the infant learning the A B C's up to the young lady of eighteen and the boy of twenty, studying

1

the highest branches taught—the three R's, 'Reading, 'Riting, 'Rithmetic. I never saw an algebra, or other mathematical work higher than the arithmetic, in Georgetown, until after I was appointed to West Point. I then bought a work on algebra in Cincinnati; but having no teacher it was Greek to me.

My father was, from my earliest recollection, in comfortable circumstances, considering the times, his place of residence, and the community in which he lived. Mindful of his own lack of facilities for acquiring an education, his greatest desire in maturer years was for the education of his children. Consequently, as stated before, I never missed a quarter from school from the time I was old enough to attend till the time of leaving home. This did not exempt me from labor. In my early days, every one labored more or less, in the region where my youth was spent, and more in proportion to their private means. It was only the very poor who were exempt. While my father carried on the manufacture of leather and worked at the trade himself, he owned and tilled considerable land. I detested the trade, preferring almost any other labor; but I was fond of agriculture, and of all employment in which horses were used. We had, among other lands, fifty acres of forest within a mile of the village. In the fall of the year choppers were employed to cut enough wood to last a twelve-month. When I was seven or eight years of age, I began hauling all the wood used in the house and shops. I could not load it on the wagons, of course, at that time, but I could drive, and the choppers would load, and some one at the house unload. When about eleven years old, I was strong enough to hold a plough. From that age until seventeen I did all the work done with horses, such as breaking up the land, furrowing, ploughing corn and potatoes, bringing in the crops when harvested, hauling all the wood, besides tending two or three horses, a cow or two, and sawing wood for stoves, etc., while still attending school. For this I was compensated by the fact that there was never any scolding or punishing by my parents; no objection to rational enjoyments, such as fishing, going to the creek a mile away to swim in summer, taking a horse and visiting my grandparents in the adjoining county, fifteen miles off, skating on the ice in winter, or taking a horse and sleigh when there was snow on the ground.

Sam Grant at West Point

When Ulysses was 17 his father obtained for him an appointment to the U. S. Military Academy at West Point. The boy had no taste for a military career, but his father's word was law and he went. He had been christened "Hiram Ulysses," but at the Academy he found that his name had been entered in the records as "Ulysses Simpson Grant." Simpson was his mother's family name and the congressman who had given him the appointment had made an understandable error in submitting the necessary papers. After a mild protest, the boy accepted the situation. Rufus Ingalls was a classmate and a close friend. Many years later, when Grant was commanding general of the armies of the United States and Ingalls was chief quartermaster in the Army of the Potomac, the staff heard a first-hand account of their chief as a cadet.

A staff-officer inquired of Ingalls whether General Grant, when at West Point, gave any promise of his future greatness. Ingalls replied: "Grant was such a quiet, unassuming fellow when a cadet that nobody would have picked him out as one who was destined to occupy a conspicuous place in history; and yet he had certain qualities which attracted attention and commanded the respect of all those in the corps with him. He was always frank, generous, and manly. At cavalry drill he excelled every one in his class. He used to take great delight in mounting and breaking in the most intractable of the new horses that were purchased from time to time and put in the squad. He succeeded in this, not by punishing the animal he had taken in hand, but by patience and tact, and his skill in making the creature know what he wanted to have it do. He was a particularly daring jumper. In jumping hurdles, when Grant's turn came the soldiers in attendance would, at an indication from him, raise the top bar a foot or so higher than usual, and he would generally manage to clear it. In his studies he was lazy and careless. Instead of studying a lesson, he would merely read it over once or twice; but he was so quick in his perceptions that he usually made very fair recitations even with so little preparation. His memory was not at all good in an attempt to learn anything by heart accurately, and this made his grade low in those branches of study which required a special effort of the memory. In scientific subjects he was very bright, and if he had labored hard he would have stood very high in them. Our class had sixty members the first year, but eight failed to pass the examinations, and the number was reduced to fifty-two. The second year's course had in it the hardest mathematics; Grant's grade in that branch was number ten. The next year he stood fifteen in natural philosophy, which stumped so many of us, and in the graduating year he was sixteen in engineering, the principal study in the first-class course. He was rather slouchy and unmilitary at infantry drills, and received about the average number of demerits. The principal reputation he gained among his fellow-cadets was for common sense, good judgment, entire unselfishness, and absolute fairness in everything he did. When we would get into an excited dispute over any subject, it was a very common thing to say, 'Well, suppose we see what Sam Grant has to say about it,' and leave it to his decision. He had been given the nickname of 'Uncle Sam' from his initials, and this was often shortened into 'Sam.' As I said, while he has not by any means conspicuous in the class, and never sought to be, he had enough marked characteristics to prevent him from being considered commonplace, and every one associated with him was sure to remember him and retain a high regard for him.''

Horace Porter, *Campaigning with Grant*

Pride Goeth Before a Fall

Grant's standing in his class at graduation from West Point in 1843 was not high enough to make him eligible for appointment to the engineers or the artillery. With his love of horses, he therefore applied for a commission in the dragoons, with the infantry as second choice. The graduating class received leave of absence for the rest of the summer and Grant went home to Bethel, Ohio, where his father had recently moved from Georgetown.

aving made alternate choice of two different arms of service with different uniforms, I could not get a uniform suit until notified of my assignment. I left my measurement with a tailor, with directions not to make the uniform until I notified him whether it was to be for infantry or dragoons. Notice did not reach me for several weeks, and then it took at least a week to get the letter of instructions to the tailor and two more to make the clothes and have them sent to me. This was a time of great suspense. I was impatient to get on my uniform and see how it looked, and probably wanted my old school-mates, particularly the girls, to see me in it.

The conceit was knocked out of me by two little circumstances that happened soon after the arrival of the clothes, which gave me a distaste for military uniform that I never recovered from. Soon after the arrival of the suit I donned it, and put off for Cincinnati on horseback. While I was riding along a street of that city, imagining that everyone was looking at me, with a feeling akin to mine when I first saw General Scott, a little urchin, bareheaded, barefooted, with dirty and ragged pants held up by a single gallows— that's what suspenders were called then—and a shirt that had not seen a wash-tub for weeks, turned to me and cried: "Soldier! will you work? No, sir-ee; I'll sell my shirt first!!" . . .

The other circumstance occurred at home. Opposite our house in Bethel stood the old stage tavern where "man and beast" found accommodation. The stable-man was rather dissipated, but possessed of some humor. On my return I found him parading the streets, and attending in the stable, barefooted, but in a pair of sky-blue nankeen pantaloons—just the color of my uniform trousers—with a strip of white cotton sheeting sewed down the outside seams in imitation of mine. The joke was a huge one in the mind of many of the people, and was much enjoyed by them; but I did not appreciate it so highly.

Personal Memoirs of U. S. Grant.

"White Haven," *the Dent country home in St. Louis County, Missouri, as it appears today. Courtesy, Missouri Historical Society, St. Louis.*

The Lieutenant Falls in Love

Fred Dent, a cadet from Missouri, had been Grant's roommate during his last year at West Point. When Grant was assigned to the 4th Infantry at Jefferson Barracks, a few miles down the Mississippi from St. Louis, Fred urged him to ride over to White Haven, the Dent country home in St. Louis County, and meet the family. He was warmly received and soon made a habit of his visits. There were two daughters in the house, Nellie, aged 15, and Emma, aged 7. Julia, then 17, was spending the winter with relatives in St. Louis. It was Emma who had first met the young lieutenant at the gate. She thought him very handsome and fell in love with him. A long time afterward she told the story of what happened next.

Then Sister Julia came home. She had already heard of the Lieutenant through the letters of my mother, who liked him very much. Quite to the contrary of the usual course under such circumstances, Julia appeared to like the young soldier also from the first moment they met. As for Lieutenant Grant—I have heard him say since that with him it was a case of love at first sight. His attentions certainly seemed to indicate it. He also told me once, when he was in the White House, that he had never had but one love affair, but the one sweetheart in his life. Not even the boyish amours that usually precede a young man's real passion had ever been his. His wife was the lady of his dreams; the heroine of his romance.

At the time Lieutenant Grant met her sister Julia was as dainty a little creature as one would care to see. She was not exactly a beauty, a slight defect of one of her eyes marring the harmony of her features, but she was possessed of a lively and pleasing countenance. Aside from this cast in her eye she was very prettily made, indeed, and was considered to have an exquisite figure. She was plump, but neither tall nor stout, and she had the slimmest, prettiest foot and hand I have ever seen on any woman, while her arms were beautifully rounded. Her hair and eyes were brown, and she had a rosy complexion that would be the envy of most girls of today.

But, to get back to their first acquaintance, the visits of the young army officer to our house became even more frequent after Julia came home. He rode over from the barracks perhaps as often as four times a week and was always pressed to stay to supper by my hospitable mother. He never seemed to require too much pressing, however; it did not take Nell and myself long to see that we were no more the attractions at White Haven for Lieutenant Grant. He showed a very quiet but marked preference for Julia's company, which only she pretended not to notice. There was nothing of the 'gushy' in his attentions to her, however, in fact, Julia was not the sort of girl to encourage that kind of thing, and what with four teasing brothers and two younger sisters on hand constantly, life would have been made something of a burden for her if she had. Their conduct toward each other was always frank and unaffected; in fact, their whole manner toward each other was that of a boy and a girl who are friends and not ashamed to show their liking for each other. There was little of the sentimental about either of them.

Emma Dent Casey, *"When Grant Went a'Courtin'"*.

Julia Dent, wife of U. S. Grant. *Collections of the Library of Congress.*

"I Shall Cling to You"

In the spring of 1844 Grant's regiment was ordered to Louisiana. The young man determined to have an understanding with Julia before he left. It was not until after his death that Mrs. Grant gave to the public her version of how he proposed.

One summer day we were going to a morning wedding, and Lieutenant Grant was also invited. He came for us on horseback, and asked my brother's permission to drive me, in exchange for his saddle, to which he gladly consented. The day was beautiful, the roads were a little heavy from previous rain, but the sun shone in splendor. We had to cross a little bridge that spanned a ravine, and, when we reached it I was surprised and a little concerned to find the gulch swollen, a most unusual thing, the water reaching to the bridge. I noticed, too, that Lieutenant Grant was very quiet, and that and the high water bothered me. I asked several times if he thought the water dangerous to breast, and told him I would go back rather than take any risk. He assured me, in his brief way, that it was perfectly safe, and in my heart I relied upon him. Just as we reached the old bridge I said, "Now if anything happens, remember I shall cling to you, no matter what you say to the contrary." He simply said, "All right," and we were over the planks in less than a minute. Then his mood changed, he became more social, and in asking me to be his wife, used my threat as a theme. After dinner that afternoon, Lieutenant Grant asked me to set the day. I wanted to be engaged, and told him it would be much nicer than getting married—a sentiment he did not approve. We were very quiet at the house that evening and neither said a word of the secret. After supper he went back to the regiment, and a few days later General Taylor sent him to Camp Salubrity, in Louisiana. He was too shy to ask father, so he waited till he was stationed and wrote to him. Father never answered the letter. I was his favorite daughter and he thought army life would not suit me.

"Besides," said father, "you are too young and the boy is too poor. He hasn't anything to give you."

I rose in my wrath and I said I was poor, too, and hadn't anything to give him.

The next year he came back on a leave of absence, and I can remember just how he looked as he rode up in his new uniform. Father was going to Washington on business, and we were all on the front porch kissing him good-by and stuffing his pockets with notes of things he was to buy. Lieutenant Grant asked for my hand, and he, in a hurry to get off, consented.

My soldier lover was in and about Mexico for four years, including the war. Every mail brought me a letter. Every one of them full of sweet nothings, love and war, and now and then some pressed flowers. Some were written on drum-heads captured from the Mexicans and others on sheets of foolscap, folded and sealed with red wafers. I read each one every day until the next one came. I have them all.

Ladies' Home Journal, October 1890.

The Belfry of San Cosme

The 4th Infantry formed a part of General Zachary Taylor's army on the Rio Grande when war with Mexico began in the spring of 1846. Grant took part in all the earlier battles of Taylor's campaign, distinguishing himself at Monterey. The regiment was then transferred to General Winfield Scott's force, assembled for an invasion of Mexico by way of Vera Cruz. As regimental quartermaster, Lieutenant Grant's proper station was in the rear with the wagon train, but whenever the regiment was in action he was found in line.

Advance along an Aqueduct in the final assault on Mexico City. *From a contemporary painting by James Walker. Courtesy, Office, Chief of Military History, U. S. Army photograph.*

During the final assault on Mexico City, the 4th Infantry and other troops advanced along a road and an arched aqueduct leading to the San Cosme garita, or gate, against desperate opposition. Grant's recollection of his part in the battle was still vivid when he wrote his Memoirs.

West of the road from where we were, stood a house occupying the southwest angle made by the San Cosme road and the road we were moving upon. A stone wall ran from the house along each of these roads for a considerable distance and thence back until it joined, enclosing quite a yard about the house. I watched my opportunity and skipped across the road and behind the south wall. Proceeding cautiously to the west corner of the enclosure, I peeped around and seeing nobody, continued, still cautiously, until the road running east and west was reached. I then returned to the troops, and called for volunteers. All that were close to me, or that heard me, about a dozen, offered their services. Commanding them to carry their arms at a trail, I watched our opportunity and got them across the road and under cover of the wall beyond, before the enemy had a shot at us. Our men under cover of the arches kept a close watch on the intrenchments that crossed our path and the house-tops beyond, and whenever a head showed itself above the parapets they would fire at it. Our crossing was thus made practicable without loss.

When we reached a safe position I instructed my little command again to carry their arms at a trail, not to fire at the enemy until they were ordered, and to move very cautiously following me until the San Cosme road was reached; we would then be on the flank of the men serving the gun on the road, and with no obstruction between us and them. When we reached the south-west corner of the enclosure before described, I saw some United States troops pushing north through a shallow ditch nearby, who had come up since my reconnaissance. This was the company of Captain Horace Brooks, of the artillery, acting as infantry. I explained to Brooks briefly what I had discovered and what I was about to do. He said, as I knew the ground and he did not, I might go on and he would follow. As soon as we got on the road leading to the city the troops serving the gun on the parapet retreated, and those on the house-tops nearby followed; our men went after them in such close pursuit—the troops we had left under the arches joining—that a second line across the road, about half-way between the first and the garita, was carried. No reinforcements had yet come up except Brooks's company, and the position we had taken was too advanced to be held by so small a force. It was given up, but retaken later in the day, with some loss.

Worth's command gradually advanced to the front now open to it. Later in the day in reconnoitring I found a church off to the south of the road, which looked to me as if the belfry would command the ground back of the garita San Cosme. I got an officer of the voltigeurs, with a mountain howitzer and men to work it, to go with me. The road being in possession of the enemy, we had to take the field to the south to reach the church. This took us over several ditches breast deep in water and grown up with water plants. These ditches, however, were not over eight or ten feet in width. The howitzer was taken to pieces and carried by the men to its destination. When I knocked for admission a priest came to the door, who, while extremely polite, declined to admit us. With the little Spanish then at my command, I explained to him that he might save property by opening the door, and he certainly would save himself from becoming a prisoner, for a time at least; and besides, I intended to go in whether he consented or not. He began to see his duty in the same light that I did, and opened the door, though he did not look as if it gave him special pleasure to do so.

The gun was carried to the belfry and put together. We were not more than two or three hundred yards from San Cosme. The shots from our little gun dropped in upon the enemy and created great confusion. Why they did not send out a small party and capture us, I do not know. We had no infantry or other defenses besides our one gun.

The effect of this gun upon the troops about the gate of the city was so marked that General Worth saw it from his position. He was so pleased that he sent a staff officer, Lieutenant Pemberton—later Lieutenant-General commanding the defenses of Vicksburg—to bring me to him. He expressed his gratification at the services the howitzer in the church steeple was doing, saying that every shot was effective, and ordered a captain of voltigeurs to report to me with another howitzer to be placed along with the one already rendering so much service. I could not tell the General that there was not room enough in the steeple for another gun, because he probably would have looked upon such a statement as a contradiction from a second lieutenant. I took the captain with me, but did not use his gun.

Personal Memoirs of U. S. Grant.

Soldier's Wedding

When the war was over and the 4th Infantry returned to the States, Grant, now a brevet captain with the permanent rank of first lieutenant, took two months' leave and went to claim his bride. He and Julia were married in the Dent family town house in St. Louis, August 22, 1848. It was a simple wedding, attended by family friends and by old West Point and Mexican War comrades of Grant's. Among these comrades were James Longstreet and Cadmus Wilcox, later distinguished soldiers of the Confederacy. Long afterward, a friend of Julia's described the event.

The bride's dress was rarely beautiful; and her lovable character and sweet ways made her as much loved as she was admired. I loved Miss Julia so dearly that I was very observant of Lieutenant Grant, though I had met him before. He was a little brown from his three years in the Mexican War, but this made him look more the soldier; and, as he stood beside his bride, clasping her hand (the smallest hand I ever saw on a woman), he in full uniform, I thought I had never seen a better embodiment of a soldier, nor a more charming wedding, although I had attended the marriage of a number of military officers. Grant's bearing was admirable; he was dignified and polite, with a marked quiet and frank naturalness.

The wedding was attended by a select few of the best people of the city, and the feeling was general that we had never seen two young persons wedded who seemed so happy and so entirely suited to a happy married life. I remember that when I kissed the bride good-bye, I whispered in her ear and told her how greatly I admired her husband, and I did, indeed, admire him.

Midland Monthly, June 1897.

The Panama Crossing

While most of the little Regular Army was stationed in the West after the war with Mexico, the 4th Infantry was assigned to the Canadian border. Grant and his bride spent the first four years of their married life in junior officers' quarters in barracks at Detroit and Sackets Harbor. In 1852 the regiment was ordered to the Pacific Coast. It was a long, hard journey, by way of Panama. There was now a two-year-old child in the household and another on the way. The Grants decided that Julia should not go, though some soldiers' wives with small children accompanied the troops. The entire regiment assembled at Governors Island, New York, for transportation to the West Coast. The side-wheeled steamer Ohio, which carried the 4th Infantry to Aspinwall, on the Isthmus of Panama, was further crowded with gold-seekers on their way to the mines of California. Lieutenant Grant was still the regimental quartermaster. His duties on board the transport were onerous; worse awaited him at the Isthmus, as he recalled when he was writing the Memoirs.

In the summer of 1852 the Panama railroad was completed only to the point where it now crosses the Chagres River. From there passengers were carried by boats to Gorgona, at which place they took mules for Panama, some twenty-five miles further. Those who travelled over the Isthmus in those days will remember that boats on the Chagres River were propelled by natives not inconveniently burdened with clothing. These boats carried thirty to forty passengers each. The crews consisted of six men to a boat, armed with long poles. There were planks wide enough for a man to walk on conveniently, running along the sides of each boat from end to end. The men would start from the bow, place one end of their poles against the river bottom, brace their shoulders against the other end, and then walk to the stern as rapidly as they could. In this way from a mile to a mile and a half an hour could be made, against the current of the river.

I, as regimental quartermaster, had charge of the public property and had also to look after the transportation. A contract had been entered into with the steamship company in New York for the transportation of the regiment to California, including the Isthmus transit. A certain amount of baggage was allowed per man, and saddle animals were to be furnished to commissioned officers and to all disabled persons. The regiment, with the exception of one company left as guards to the public property—camp and garrison equipage principally—and the soldiers with families, took boats, propelled as above described, for Gorgona. From this place they marched to Panama, and were soon comfortably on the steamer anchored in the bay, some three or four miles from the town. I, with one company of troops and all the soldiers with families, all the tents, mess chests and camp kettles, was sent to Cruces, a town a few miles higher up the Chagres River than Gorgona. There I found an impecunious American who had taken the contract to furnish transportation for the regiment at a stipulated price per hundred pounds for the freight and so much for each saddle animal. But when we reached Cruces there was not a mule, either for pack or saddle, in the place. The contractor promised that the animals should be on hand in the morning. In the morning he said that they were on the way from some imaginary place, and would arrive in the course of the day. This went on until I saw that he could not procure the animals at all at the price he had promised to furnish them for. The unusual number of passengers that had come over on the steamer, and the large amount of freight to pack, had created an unprecedented demand for mules. Some of the passengers paid as high as forty dollars for the use of a mule to ride twenty-five miles, when the mule would not have sold for ten dollars in that market at other times. Meanwhile the cholera had broken out, and men were dying every hour. To diminish the food for the disease, I permitted the company detailed with me to proceed to Panama. The captain and the doctors accompanied the men, and I was left alone with the sick and the soldiers who had families. The regiment at Panama was also affected with the disease; but there were better accommodations for the well on the steamer, and a hospital, for those taken with the disease, on an old hulk anchored a mile off. There were also hospital tents on shore on the island of Flamingo, which stands in the bay.

I was about a week at Cruces before transportation began to come in. About one-third of the people with me died, either at Cruces or on the way to Panama. There was no agent of the transportation company at Cruces to consult, or to take the responsibility of procuring transportation at a price which would secure it. I therefore myself dismissed the contractor and made a new contract with a native, at more than double the original price. Thus we finally reached Panama. The steamer, however, could not proceed until the cholera abated, and the regiment was detained still longer. Altogether, on the Isthmus and on the Pacific side, we were delayed six weeks. About one-seventh of those who left New York harbor with the 4th Infantry on the 5th of July, now lie buried on the Isthmus of Panama or on Flamingo Island in Panama Bay.

Leaving the Army

Prices were very high on the Pacific Coast and Grant soon found that on his Army pay he would be unable to bring Julia and the children, one of whom he had never seen, to join him. At Fort Vancouver on the Columbia River, his first duty station, he tried various ways of supplementing his salary. They all turned out badly. Promotion to captain's rank did not solve the problem. Transfer to Fort Humboldt in northern California involved giving up the assignment as regimental quartermaster, which had kept him busy, and taking command of a small company, diminished by desertion to the gold fields. His duties at this isolated outpost were reduced to a dull routine. Lonely, homesick and bored, he determined to leave the service.

Grant submitted his resignation on the day his commission as captain arrived from Washington, and it was accepted without comment by his commanding officer. A story circulated in the little Regular Army afterward that his resignation had been precipitated by trouble with this officer, who had a reputation as a rigid disciplinarian, over his drinking. This story was revived during the Civil War and gained wide credence. But there is nothing in the official records to indicate that Grant's resignation was anything but voluntary. His letters to Julia from Fort Humboldt indicate that the separation from her and from the children was becoming unendurable. The idea of throwing up his commission and going home had long been in his mind.

March 6, 1854: I have only one letter from you in three months, and that had been a long time on the way. I know there are letters for me in the Post Office somewhere, but when shall I get them? I sometimes get so anxious to see you, and our little boys, that I am almost tempted to resign and trust to Providence, and my exertions, for a living where I can have you and them with me. It would only require the certainty of a moderate competency to make me take this step. . . .

March 25: I have had just one solitary letter from you since I arrived at this place and that was written about October of last year.

I cannot believe that you have neglected to write all this time but it does seem hard that I should not hear from you. I am afraid too that many of my letters do not reach you. The only way of mailing them is to give them to a captain of a vessel to put them in the Post Office in San Francisco, which, if he does, they are all safe, but I have no doubt but that many times they never spend a second thought about letters entrusted to them.

April 3: . . . How very anxious I am to get home again. I do not feel as if it were possible to endure this separation much longer. But how do I know that you are thinking as much of me as I am of you? I do not get letters to tell me so. But you write, I am certain, and some day I will get a big batch all at once. Just think, by the time you receive this Ulys will be nearly two years old and no doubt talking as plainly as Fred did his few words when I saw him last. . . .

Grant Family Papers.

"Hardscrabble," *the log house or "cabin" which the Grants built and lived in from 1856 to 1858, after he resigned from the Army. Today, it is located sonth of St. Louis, on "Grants Farm," the estate of August A. Busch, Jr. Courtesy, Missouri Historical Society, St. Louis.*

Hardscrabble

After his return from the Army, Grant and his family lived with the Dents at White Haven for a year. Julia's father, Colonel Frederick Dent, had given her sixty acres and Grant began clearing and cultivating this land. The only cash crop at first was firewood, which he cut and sold in St. Louis. In 1855 the Grants left White Haven and moved to Wish-ton-wish, a house built by one of Julia's brothers on his land nearby. Here their third child, a daughter, Nellie, was born. Meanwhile, Grant was cutting and seasoning logs for a house of their own on Julia's land. This house, which he named "Hardscrabble" and into which they moved in the following year, was later famous as "the Grant log cabin." But sister Emma recalled it rather romantically in her old age, and Mrs. Henry T. Blow, a St. Louis friend of the Dents, gushed over it after a visit while Julia and Ulysses were living there. It was at least their own, and they seem to have been happy in it. Here their fourth and last child, Jesse, named for Grant's father, was born.

The house that the Grants built was of logs. The logs for it were cut and shaped by the Captain himself. It was planned by Mrs. Grant, and was both fashioned and furnished with an eye to the artistic, as well as for comfort and coziness. Though not pretentious to modern eyes it was not the mean, ramshackle hut that the popular mind supposes it to have been. It had five good rooms and a hall, which furnished all the space the Grants needed at that time. I know that it was on exhibition at the World's Fair in St. Louis, and it looked anything but elegant there, amid its more garish surroundings. But it had been built fifty years before, and it had not been lived in for a great many of those years.

Emma Dent Casey, *"When Grant Went a'Courtin.'"*

I quite envy her. No grand city home can compare with that log building. It's warm in winter and cool in summer; and oh, the happy life in the very heart of nature! The spotless linen, the bits of delicate color in furnishings, the engravings on the walls, the books, reviews and magazines lying about, nowhere else look so fresh and so beautiful as in that country log cabin. It is the very expression of refinement, of culture and good taste. "Cabin" is a misnomer. It is a castle if we are allowed to estimate the structure by the happiness, the thought and the culture within it.

Midland Monthly, September 1897.

Difficult Years

Hopes of making a paying venture of farming at Hardscrabble were dimmed by the panic of 1857 and the depression that followed. Crops were hardly worth hauling to town. In 1858 Colonel Dent, now a widower, moved into his St. Louis house and left White Haven in the care of the Grants. Prospects brightened with the management of a large, developed farm, but Ulysses was stricken with ague and had to give it up. He entered a real estate firm in St. Louis, but the business was not a success. He sought an appointment as county engineer but, in spite of influential backing, failed to receive it. In 1860 he turned for help to his father, who was now living in Covington, Kentucky. Jesse Grant, Senior, at this time had an extensive leather business with a branch in Galena, Illinois, under the management of two younger sons. Ulysses had always hated the business, but now he had no choice. His father told the story a few years later to one of Grant's first biographers.

In April, 1860, Grant went to Galena, Illinois, and entered the leather store belonging to his father, and conducted by his two brothers. "He took right hold of the business with his accustomed industry," says his father, "and was a very good salesman. He had a faculty to entertain people in conversation, although he talked but little himself. But he never would take any pains to extend his acquaintance in Galena; and after he joined the army, and had begun to be distinguished, citizens of the town would stop in front of our store within six feet of the windows, and look in to see which of the Grants it was that was absent, and had become famous." In another letter addressed to the author, dated, Covington, Kentucky, March 20, 1868, he says:—"After Ulysses' farming and real estate experiments failed to be self-supporting, he came to me at this place for advice and assistance. I referred him to Simpson, my next oldest son, who had charge of my Galena business, and who was staying with me at that time on account of poor health. Simpson sent him to the Galena store to stay until something better should turn up in his favor, and told him he would allow him a salary of eight hundred dollars per annum. That amount would have supported his family then, but he owed debts at St. Louis, and did draw fifteen hundred dollars in the year, but he paid back the balance after he went into the army."

James G. Wilson, *The Life and Public Services of Ulysses Simpson Grant.*

"I Can But See the Doom of Slavery"

Within a year of Grant's arrival at Galena the Civil War broke out. He had taken little part in politics, as the dispute over slavery extension gradually deepened into a great national crisis and finally exploded in armed conflict. The Dents were slaveholders and Colonel Dent was a staunch supporter of the right of secession. With the firing on Fort Sumter and President Lincoln's call for volunteers, Grant shared the wave of patriotic fervor that swept the North. He felt impelled to let his father-in-law know just where he stood.

Galena, April 19th, 1861

Mr. F. Dent: Dear Sir—I have but little time to write, but as in these exciting times we are very anxious to hear from you, and know of no other way but by writing first to you, I must make time. We get but little news by telegraph from St. Louis, but from all other points of the country we are hearing all the time. The times are indeed startling; but now is the time particularly in the border slave State, for men to prove their love of country. I know it is hard for men to apparently work with the Republican party, but now all party distinctions should be lost sight of and every true patriot be for maintaining the integrity of the glorious old Stars and Stripes, the Constitution and the Union. The North is responding to the President's call in such a manner that the Confederates may truly quake. I tell you there is no mistaking the feelings of the people. The Government can call into the field 75,000 troops, and ten or twenty times 75,000 if it should be necessary and find the means of maintaining them, too. It is all a mistake about the Northern pocket being so sensitive. In times like the present no people are more ready to give their own time or of their abundant means. No impartial man can conceal from himself the fact that in all these troubles the Southerners have been the aggressors, and the administration has stood purely on the defensive—more on the defensive than she would dared to have done, but for her consciousness of strength and the certainty of right prevailing in the end.

The news to-day is that Virginia has gone out of the Union. But for the influence she will have on the other border States, this is not much to be regretted. Her position, or rather that of eastern Virginia, has been more reprehensible from the beginning than that of South Carolina. She should be made to bear a heavy portion of the burden of the war for her guilt.

In all this I can but see the doom of slavery. The Northerners do not want, nor will they want, to interfere with the institution, but they will refuse for all time to give it protection, unless the Southerners shall return soon to their allegiance, and then, too, this disturbance will give such an impetus to the production of their staple—cotton—in other parts of the world that they can never recover the control of the market again for that commodity. This will reduce the value of the negroes so much that they will never be worth fighting over again.

I have just received a letter from Fred. He breathes forth the most patriotic sentiments. He is for the old flag as long as there is a union of two States fighting under its banner, and when they dissolve he will go it alone. This is not his language, but it is the idea not so well expressed as he expresses it. Julia and the children are all well and join me in love to you all. I forgot to mention that Fred has another heir, with some novel name that I have forgotten.

Yours truly,
U. S. Grant.

Frank A. Burr, *A New, Original and Authentic Record of the Life and Deeds of General U. S. Grant.*

In June 1861 Governor Yates appointed Grant to command the 21st Illinois Volunteer Infantry. *Reproduced through the courtesy of the Illinois State Historical Library, Springfield.*

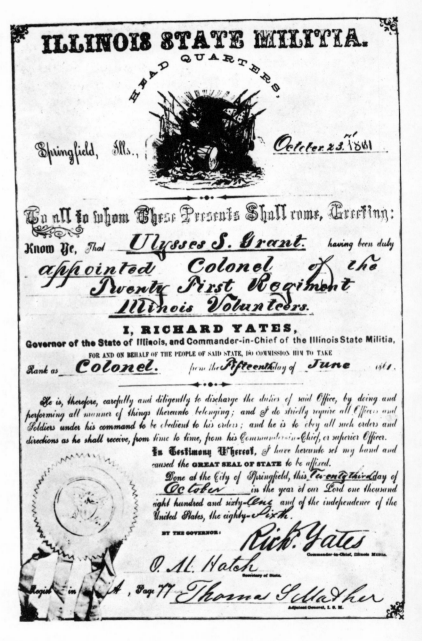

24

Governor Yates's Hellions .

While Grant was not well known in Galena, he was recognized as a man with West Point training and Mexican War experience. He was offered command of the first volunteer company raised in the town, but declined, believing himself fitted to command a regiment. His offer of service to the War Department was ignored, but the State of Illinois gave him temporary duty organizing and mustering in the new regiments being raised there. In June Governor Richard Yates appointed him to command of the 21st Illinois Volunteer Infantry, a regiment notorious for its poor discipline and embarrassingly becoming known as "Governor Yates's Hellions." This regiment Colonel Grant quickly brought into shape and it served creditably under him in Missouri. A Galena neighbor, a man of some political influence who had taken command of the local company after Grant had refused it, later recounted the circumstances of Grant's appointment as a colonel. Grant himself wrote with some pride to his father a few weeks after he had taken over the regiment.

About the 10th of June he received a telegram from Governor Yates asking if he would accept the colonelcy of the Twenty-first Illinois infantry, known as the Mattoon regiment, which he had organized and mustered into the state service the month before. He, of course, accepted the position offered. It seems that this piece of good luck came to the captain in this wise. The Mattoon regiment had been unfortunate in its choice of a colonel for the thirty days' service, who became unpopular with both officers and enlisted men before the expiration of that time, and a change was desired by all. The officers, who had made the acquaintance of Captain Grant as mustering officer, believed him to be a good man for the position and petitioned Governor Yates to appoint him colonel of the regiment. The governor hesitated, for he clearly was not partial to Captain Grant, but the Hon. Jesse K. Dubois, the state auditor, who happened to be in the governor's room when the petition was received, spoke in such high terms of the "Galena Captain," as the governor called him, and of his fitness for the position, that it turned the scales and the appointment was made.

Colonel Grant took command of the regiment at Camp Yates, Springfield, where it had been brought from Mattoon. It had been neglected by its late colonel and its drill and discipline were below par. It devolved on its new commander to raise its esprit de corps and make it what it became in the next two months, one of the most efficient regiments in the Western Army. Many stories are told how the colonel, in his quiet but firm way, subdued some of its most unruly men. He took his regiment to Missouri, where it was kept busy fighting the "bushwhackers" of that region.

Augustus L. Chetlain, *Recollections of Seventy Years.*

Mexico, Mo.
Aug. 3, 1861

Dear Father:

I have written to you once from this place and received no answer, but as Orvil writes to me that you express great anxiety to hear from me often I will try and find time to drop you a line twice a month, and oftener when anything of special interest occurs.

I see from the papers that my name has been sent in for Brigadier Gen.! This is certainly very complimentary to me particularly as I have never asked a friend to intercede in my behalf. My only acquaintance with men of influence in the State was whilst on duty at Springfield, and I then saw such pulling and hauling for favors I determined never to ask for anything, and never have, not even a Colonelcy. I wrote a letter to Washington tendering my services but then declined Gov. Yates' & Mr. Trumbull's endorsement.

My services with the Regt. I am now with have been highly satisfactory to me. I took it in a very disorganized, demoralized, and insubordinate condition and have worked it up to a reputation equal to the best, and I believe with the good will of all the officers and all the men. Hearing that I was likely to be promoted the officers, with great unanimity, have requested to be attached to my Command. This I don't want you to read to others for I very much dislike speaking of myself.

Yours truly,

U. S. Grant.

U. S. Grant Papers, Missouri Historical Society.

The Other Fellow is Scared, Too

Grant's command of a regiment was brief, but it was an important step in his higher military education. One lesson that he learned during this period he recounted with some humor in the Memoirs.

I took my regiment to Palmyra and remained there for a few days, until relieved by the 19th Illinois infantry. From Palmyra I proceeded to Salt River, the railroad bridge over which had been destroyed by the enemy. Colonel John M. Palmer at that time commanded the 13th Illinois, which was acting as a guard to workmen who were engaged in rebuilding this bridge. Palmer was my senior and commanded the two regiments as long as we remained together. The bridge was finished in about two weeks, and I received orders to move against Colonel Thomas Harris, who was said to be encamped at the little town of Florida, some twenty-five miles south of where we then were.

At the time of which I now write we had no transportation and the country about Salt River was sparsely settled, so that it took some days to collect teams and drivers enough to move the camp and garrison equipage of a regiment nearly a thousand strong, together with a week's supply of provision and some ammunition. While preparations for the move were going on I felt quite comfortable; but when we got on the road and found every house deserted I was anything but easy. In the twenty-five miles we had to march we did not see a person, old or young, male or female, except two horsemen who were on a road that crossed ours. As soon as they saw us they decamped as fast as their horses could carry them. I kept my men in the ranks and forbade their entering any of the deserted houses or taking anything from them. We halted at night on the road and proceeded the next morning at an early hour. Harris had been encamped in a creek bottom for the sake of being near water. The hills on either side of the creek extend to a considerable height, possibly more than a hundred feet. As we approached the brow of the hill from which it was expected we could see Harris' camp, and possibly find his men ready formed to meet us, my heart kept getting higher and higher until it felt to me as though it was in my throat. I would have given anything then to have been back in Illinois, but I had not the moral courage to halt and consider what to do; I kept right on. When we reached a point from which the valley below was in full view I halted. The place where Harris had been encamped a few days before was still there and the marks of a recent encampment were plainly visible, but the troops were gone. My heart resumed its place. It occurred to me at once that Harris had been as much afraid of me as I had been of him. This was a view of the question I had never taken before; but it was one I never forgot afterwards. From that event to the close of the war, I never experienced trepidation upon confronting an enemy, though I always felt more or less anxiety. I never forgot that he had as much reason to fear my forces as I had his. The lesson was valuable.

Personal Memoirs of U. S. Grant.

The new Brigadier General at Cairo, Illinois. *Collections of the Library of Congress.*

The New Brigadier General

Soon after his promotion to the rank of brigadier general, Grant was assigned to command at Cairo, Illinois. Here, at the junction of the Mississippi and Ohio Rivers, was a natural point of departure for any advance against the Confederacy in the West. Major John H. Brinton, a medical officer attached to his command at this time, has left an interesting picture of the new general. When Brinton reported for duty at Cairo, Dr. Simons, the medical director, advised him to take board in the same home with the rest of the staff, over Safford's Bank.

By this he meant that the general and the staff boarded in the house, and I then found out that the lower story, the back offices in fact, or a part of them were occupied by Brigadier General U. S. Grant, U.S.V., as headquarters. I was at once introduced to the general, who, I believed, had only a few days previous received his brigadier general's commission.

Of the many who have written of him, made speeches about him, applauded him, and flattered him, few, very few are left who saw him, and watched him, and studied him, as I did. From the very first, he attracted me, and I felt very soon, and indeed at the time of the battle of Belmont, Mo., wrote home, that the man had come who would finish this war, should he have the chance.

I first saw General Grant at the dinner table, when I was introduced to him by Dr. Simons, receiving from him a friendly nod. On the same evening I went into the bank. Behind the counter, the general and his assistant adjutant general, Jno. A. Rawlins, or Captain Rawlins, as he was then, were seated at a little round table. I fancy that I wanted to write a letter home, for I remember that the general very kindly asked me to sit down, and continued his work with Rawlins. I had then a good opportunity to observe him, and I did so very closely. He was then a very different looking man from the General Grant, or the President of after days. As I first saw him, he was a very short, small, rather spare man with full beard and moustache. His beard was a little long, very much longer than he afterwards wore it, unkempt and irregular, and of a sandy, tawny shade. His hair matched his beard, and at a first glance he seemed to be a very ordinary sort of a man, indeed one below the average in most respects. But as I sat and watched him then, and many an hour afterwards, I found that his face grew upon me. His eyes were gentle with a kind expression, and thoughtful. He did not as a rule, speak a great deal. At that time he seemed to be turning matters over in his mind, and to be very much occupied indeed with the work of the hour. He did nothing carelessly, but worked slowly, every now and then stopping and taking his pipe out of his mouth.

But this reminds me, that I have not yet spoken of his pipe. The man in after days became so thoroughly identified with the cigar, that people could scarcely believe that he was once an assiduous smoker of the pipe. Well, the pipe which he first used was a meerschaum with a curved stem eight or nine inches long, which allowed the pipe to hang down. He smoked steadily and slowly and evidently enjoyed his tobacco.

I have already referred to General Grant's friendly treatment. I find in a letter to Dr. DaCosta, dated Nov. 20th, 1861, this allusion:

"General Grant (an old regular) is very kind to me and helps me out of many a tight place. So also does Captain Hawkins (regular). We are quite intimate. Grant is a plain, straight forward, peremptory and prompt man. If I ask for anything it is done at once, the great secret in all military matters."

Personal Memoirs of John H. Brinton

Unconditional Surrender

Grant's capture of Forts Henry and Donelson, on the Tennessee and Cumberland Rivers just south of the Kentucky line, was the first important victory for the Union arms. This campaign, in February, 1862, brought Grant to national attention and made him the hero of the hour in the North. The Confederates in Fort Donelson had made a vigorous counterattack on the Union lines the day before their surrender, and the right of Grant's army under General John McClernand had been driven back in confusion. General Lew Wallace, who took part in the action, thought later that this was one of the great crises in Grant's military career.

Just then General Grant rode up to where General McClernand and I were in conversation. He was almost unattended.

In his hand there were some papers, which looked like telegrams. Wholly unexcited, he saluted and received the salutations of his subordinates. Proceeding at once to business, he directed them to retire their commands to the heights out of cannon range, and throw up works. Reinforcements were *en route*, he said, and it was advisable to await their coming. He was then informed of the mishap to the First Division, and that the road to Charlotte was open to the enemy.

In every great man's career there is a crisis exactly similar to that which now overtook General Grant, and it cannot be better described than as a crucial test of his nature. A mediocre person would have accepted the news as an argument for persistence in his resolution to enter upon a siege. Had General Grant done so, it is very probable his history would have been then and there concluded. His admirers and detractors are alike invited to study him at this precise juncture. It cannot be doubted that he saw with painful distinctness the effect of the disaster to his right wing. His face flushed slightly. With a sudden grip he crushed the papers in his hand. But in an instant these signs of disappointment or hesitation—as the reader pleases—cleared away. In his ordinary quiet voice he said, addressing himself to both officers,

Newspapers from home.

"Gentlemen, the position on the right must be retaken." With that he turned and galloped off.

When Grant left Wallace and McClernand it was to order an immediate attack by General Charles F. Smith's division on the left. This attack brought the capture of the outer line of the Confederate earthworks and foreshadowed complete success. The enemy decided to surrender rather than face an overwhelming assault. The terms that Grant gave to the Confederate commander became famous. He was hailed as "Unconditional Surrender" Grant, a play upon his initials and the terms that he offered his opponent. Grant included in his Memoirs the exchange of letters leading to the surrender.

Before daylight General Smith brought to me the following letter from General Buckner:

> Headquarters, Fort Donelson,
> February 16, 1862.

Sir: — In consideration of all the circumstances governing the present situation of affairs at this station, I propose to the Commanding Officer of the Federal forces the appointment of Commissioners to agree upon terms of capitulation of the forces and fort under my command, and in that view suggest an armistice until 12 o'clock to-day.

> I am, sir, very respectfully,
> Your ob't se'v't,
> S. B. Buckner,
> Brig. Gen. C.S.A.

To Brigadier-General U. S. Grant,
    Com'ding U. S. Forces,
        Near Fort Donelson.

To this I responded as follows:

> Headquarters Army in the Field,
> Camp Near Donelson,
> February 16, 1862.

General S. B. Buckner,
    Confederate Army.

Sir: — Yours of this date, proposing armistice and appointment of Commissioners to settle terms of capitulation, is just received. No terms except an unconditional and immediate surrender can be accepted. I propose to move immediately upon your works.

I am, sir, very respectfully,
Your ob't se'v't,
U. S. Grant,
Brig. Gen.

To this I received the following reply:

Headquarters, Dover, Tennessee,
February 16, 1862.

To Brig. Gen'l U. S. Grant,
    U. S. Army.
Sir: — The distribution of the forces under my command, incident to an unexpected change of commanders, and the overwhelming force under your command, compel me, notwithstanding the brilliant success of the Confederate arms yesterday, to accept the ungenerous and unchivalrous terms which you propose.

I am, sir,
Your very ob't se'v't,
S. B. Buckner,
Brig. Gen. C.S.A.

Personal Memoirs of U. S. Grant.

How Grant Became A Cigar Smoker

The victory at Donelson not only made Grant a major general and a popular hero, but it also resulted in a change in his personal habits. It was late in the war when he told his staff how he happened to take up cigar smoking. One night early in 1865 the Confederate gunboats came down from Richmond and threatened to get within shelling distance of the Union base at City Point on the James River. It was a critical moment and headquarters was a busy place until it passed.

On the morning of January 24 breakfast in the mess-room was a little later than usual, as every one had been trying to make up for the sleep lost the previous night. When the chief had lighted his cigar after the morning meal, and taken his place by the camp-fire, a staff-officer said: "General, I never saw cigars consumed quite so rapidly as those you smoked last night when you were writing despatches to head off the ironclads." He smiled, and remarked: "No; when I come to think of it, those cigars didn't last very long, did they?" An allusion was then made to the large number he had smoked the second day of the battle of the Wilderness. In reply to this he said: "I had been a very light smoker previous to the attack on Donelson, and after that battle I acquired a fondness for cigars by reason of a purely accidental circumstance. Admiral Foote, commanding the fleet of gunboats which were cooperating with the army, had been wounded, and at his request I had gone aboard his flag-ship to confer with him. The admiral offered me a cigar, which I smoked on my way back to my headquarters. On the road I was met by a staff-officer, who announced that the enemy were making a vigorous attack. I galloped forward at once, and while riding among the troops giving directions for repulsing the assault I carried the cigar in my hand. It had gone out, but it seems that I continued to hold the stump between my fingers throughout the battle. In the ac-

35

counts published in the papers I was represented as smoking a cigar in the midst of the conflict; and many persons, thinking, no doubt, that tobacco was my chief solace, sent me boxes of the choicest brands from everywhere in the North. As many as ten thousand were soon received. I gave away all I could get rid of, but having such a quantity on hand, I naturally smoked more than I would have done under ordinary circumstances, and I have continued the habit ever since."

Horace Porter, Campaigning with Grant.

"Going into bivouac at night."

Bloody Shiloh

The two-day battle of Shiloh, or Pittsburg Landing, Tennessee, was fought in early April, 1862. The Union forces under Grant's command finally gained the victory, after a near disaster. It was the first great battle of the Civil War, and one of the bloodiest. North America had never seen such slaughter. The people of the North were shocked by the casualty lists and sought a victim to assuage their grief. The commanding general, only recently their hero, was the logical sacrifice. Grant, after this victory, was more

*ferociously assailed in the press and in the halls of Congress than
were many defeated generals later in the war. One of his staff officers, having been urgently asked for the facts, gave his account of
the battle in a private letter to his questioner.*

Head Quarters Army in the Field
Near Pittsburg Tenn. April 19th 1862.

E. Hempstead Esqr

Dear Sir   Yours of the 14th Inst is just recd and I will proceed at once to answer your enquiries on the score of old friendship. First as to the Genls being *intemperate*. I pronounce it an un-
mitigated slander. I have been on his staff ever since the Donelson
affair (and saw him frequently during that) and necessary in close
contact with him *every day*, and I have never seen him take even
a glass of liquor more than two or three times in my life and then
only a single one at a time, and have never seen him intoxicated
or even approximate to it. As to the story that he was intoxicated
at the Battle of Pittsburg, I have only to say that the man who
fabricated the story is an infamous *liar*, and you are at liberty to
say to him that I say so. As to the question was the Gen. at the
town of Savannah at the commencement of the fight, I answer he
was. There was the point where our head quarters were established
as being the most convenient for all parts of the command, some
of the troops being stationed at Crumps Landing, 4 miles above,
some at Pittsburg, and the new arrivals all coming to Savanna
made it necessary to establish Headquarters at that place, although the General was personally at Pittsburg almost every day,
and had made arrangements to remove there permanently as soon

Beef for the Troops.

37

as Buell's forces should arrive. On the morning of the 6th we embarked on the Steamer as soon as the firing commenced at Pittsburg (the distance is about 8½ miles) and we arrived there at about ½ past 7 o'clock stopping at Crump's Landing where L. Wallace & his command were encamped long enough to order his Division under arms ready to move at a moment's notice. And meeting the messenger who was sent to Savanna to notify us of the attack only two miles below Pittsburg where we arrived before the attack had become general all along the line, from which time Gen. Grant was in the saddle constantly and always, where the fight was the hottest. As to our being surprised it is simply all humbug and the sensation stories about officers and men being bayonetted in their tents would do to publish in the Ledger "to be continued" but newspapers of character ought to be ashamed to give circulation to such absurdities, as I do not believe that in truth a *single man* was killed by a bayonet during the two days fight. I did not see one, and I think I saw as much of the fight as anyone, being constantly engaged in carrying orders from one part of the field to the other. The simple statement of the whole matter is this. We were attacked by vastly superior numbers on Sunday and were crowded hard and forced gradually to contract our lines, during the whole day but at no time did we imagine that we were whipped or would be, Grant always insisting that we were able to whip them & would do it as soon as Wallace and Nelson (who had arrived at Savanna the night before) should arrive with their forces . . . they did not get in until dark in the meantime our forces were gallantly contesting the ground *inch by inch* until dark. As to the story that Prentiss was surprised I have only to say that I myself saw Prentiss after noon gallantly fighting at the head of his Division. It was I think about 2 o'clock PM when he was outflanked and himself and a part of his command captured. Most of our troops behaved *well* but some of the raw regiments broke and *run* and among them their officers. These stories you hear emanate (from them). It is necessary that they should have some excuse for their cowardice and the best way to direct public attention from themselves is to direct it in some other course. As to your question Did General Grant lead the last charge on Monday? I answer he did, as I was present and saw it, having been sent by him to bring up the troops. It was the turning point of the day and ended the close fighting. I hear nothing of the

38

Charging the "Hornet's Nest" at Shiloh. *Some of the most desperate action of the battle took place here, where Prentiss defended himself for hours against repeated Confederate attacks. Sketch from* Battles and Leaders of the Civil War.

troops having lost confidence in their Division commanders. If those newspaper correspondents who take so much pains to vilify men who are engaged in fighting the battle would shoulder a musket and go into the field themselves I think they would do more to advance the cause, than in pitching in undiscriminately as they do. So far as Gen. Grant is concerned, they are losing their time and trouble as he has no political asperations as they seem to fear and will never be a candidate for President. His greatist ambition is to see this war pushed to a close, and then go Home to his family and business. One question more I have forgotten why we were at Pittsburg in the face of the enemy not entrenched. As to the entrenchments this is a heavily timbered country and one where entrenchments amount to nothing. And we came here to fight. If we had staid at Chicago or Cairo I have no idea the fight would have taken place, but it did take place and we gave them a glorious thrashing. Col. Smith (JE) & Dr. Kittoe are both here and well.

Yours, etc.

W. R. Rowley.

Elihu B. Washburne Papers, Library of Congress.

"I Can't Spare This Man"

So loud was the clamor for Grant's removal from command after Shiloh, that Lincoln's friends became alarmed for the safety of the administration. A. K. McClure, an influential Pennsylvania Republican close to the President, has told how he tried to persuade Lincoln to remove Grant.

I did not know Grant at that time; had neither partiality nor prejudice to influence my judgment, nor had I any favorite general who might be benefited by Grant's overthrow, but I shared the almost universal conviction of the President's friends that he could not sustain himself if he attempted to sustain Grant by continuing him in command. Looking solely to the interests of Lincoln, feeling that the tide of popular resentment was so overwhelming against Grant that Lincoln must yield to it, I had repeated conferences with some of his closest friends, including Swett and Lamon, all of whom agreed that Grant must be removed from his command, and complained of Lincoln for his manifest injustice to himself by his failure to act promptly in Grant's removal. So much was I impressed with the importance of prompt action on the part of the President after spending a day and evening in Washington that I called on Lincoln at eleven o'clock at night and sat with him alone until after one o'clock in the morning. He was, as usual, worn out with the day's exacting duties, but he did not permit me to depart until the Grant matter had been gone over and many other things relating to the war that he wished to discuss. I pressed upon him with all the earnestness I could command the immediate removal of Grant as an imperious necessity to sustain himself. As was his custom, he said but little, only enough to make me continue the discussion until it was exhausted. He sat before the open fire in the old Cabinet room, most of the time with his feet up on the high marble mantel, and exhibited unusual distress at the complicated condition of military affairs. Nearly every day brought some new and perplexing military complication. He had gone through a long winter of terrible strain with McClellan and the Army of the Potomac; and from the day that Grant started on his Southern expedition until the battle of Shiloh he had had little else than jarring and confusion among his generals in the West. He knew that I had no ends to serve in urging Grant's removal, beyond the single desire to make him be just to himself, and he listened patiently.

I appealed to Lincoln for his own sake to remove Grant at once, and in giving my reasons for it I simply voiced the admittedly overwhelming protest from the loyal people of the land against Grant's continuance in command. I could form no judgment during the conversation as to what effect my arguments had upon him beyond the fact that he was greatly distressed at this new complication. When I had said everything that could be said from my standpoint, he lapsed into silence. Lincoln remained silent for what seemed a very long time. He then gathered himself up in his chair and said in a tone of earnestness that I shall never forget: *"I can't spare this man; he fights."*

A. K. McClure, *Abraham Lincoln and Men of War-Times.*

"Fall in for soup"

The Chaplain Gets a New Job

In the fall of 1862 Grant's forces were operating in western Tennessee and northern Mississippi. Many plantation owners had gone south and the Negro slaves flocked into the Union camps where, like refugees in all times, they presented a problem. In November Chaplain John Eaton, of the 27th Ohio, received an order from General Grant to take charge of these "contrabands," as they were then

41

called, organize them into companies, and put them to work picking, ginning, and baling the ungathered cotton. He was to report for further instructions. Eaton did not want to leave his regiment and his experiences with other generals and their headquarters had not been happy. He reported reluctantly.

I dismounted, hitched my horse, and approaching a sentry who paced in front of a large house, I inquired of him where General Grant was to be found. He directed me to enter the house, and, pointing to the passageway, told me that I should find the General's orderly at his door and that he would direct me. My heart was thumping violently, but I found the orderly, and asked to have him announce that Chaplain Eaton had come to report in accordance with orders. To my surprise he said,—pointing to the door before which we were standing,—"tap on the door and he'll tell you to come in." This seemed very different from my previous experiences at headquarters. I rapped, and a voice said very quietly, "Come in." Upon entering the room the same quiet voice said to me, "Have a seat, and I'll talk with you in a few moments." Then, as I announced my name, the General added, "Oh, you are the man who has all these darkies on his shoulders."

I saw at a glance that I had interrupted a council of the various generals in Grant's command, and I felt distinctly out of place. Grant, who was seated at the centre-table, was distinguished from his officers only by the shoulder-straps of a Major General. My eyes were alert for the signs on his face of the dissipation with which rumor charged him, but I saw at once that no such signs were there. Everything about him betokened moderation and simplicity. His simplicity was no less obvious than the respect which his associate generals manifested for him. I felt my preconceived notions of headquarters and the atmosphere surrounding them undergoing a change. From the concluding words of the conference it was evident that important details in connection with the projected movement on Vicksburg had been under discussion. The officers soon filed out, and as they passed me, one and another threw me a glance of amused comprehension, as if they had some suspicion of what my duties were to be. When the last one had left the room, Grant turned to me, and pointing to the table at which he was seated said, "Sit up, and we'll talk." I drew my chair to his table, hardly knowing whether I was the same man who had ridden into camp with such unpleasant memories of former experiences with our commanders and such dark forebodings of the experience before me.

An earnest conversation followed, which though it involved me in great responsibilities, relieved my mind once and for all of my anxiety concerning the man to whom I had come to report. At first I exerted myself to the utmost to have the order which had brought me revoked. I described the situation in the brigade, where, in the absence of so many chaplains, I had been able to become active and helpful among a large body of soldiers. I emphasized my inability, lacking as I was in commanding rank, to enforce the orders I should find it necessary to issue. To take the colored people out of the camps would bring me into conflict with all the officers now making personal use of their services; to set them at work in the cotton fields, the product of which was to be turned over to the

The "barber" in camp.

Government, would bring me into conflict with all the speculators in the cotton interest. The price of cotton was then mounting, and speculation ran high. I felt so intensely my own inability to meet the situation that I put forward all the energy I could summon to get the order revoked. All that I said had no more effect upon that quiet, attentive face than a similar appeal might have had upon a stone wall. When my arguments were exhausted, the General simply remarked, "Mr. Eaton, I have ordered you to report to me in person, and I will take care of you." And so he did.

John Eaton, *Grant, Lincoln and the Freedmen: Reminiscences of the Civil War.*

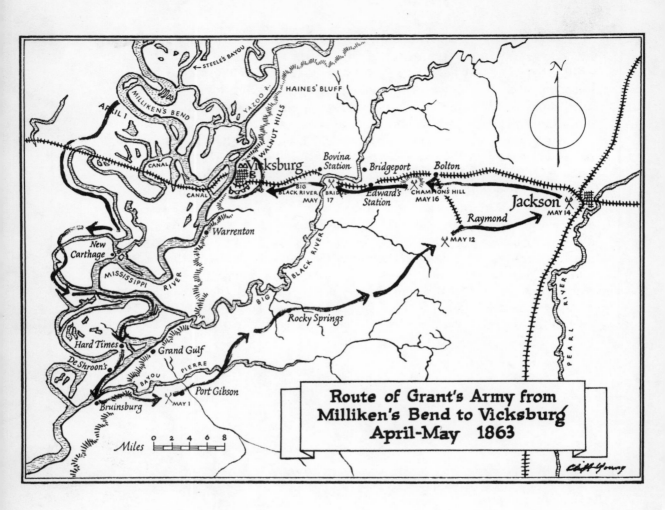

STEELE'S BAYOU

MILLIKEN'S BEND

APRIL 1

HAINES' BLUFF

YAZOO R.

WALNUT HILLS

CANAL

Vicksburg

Bovina Station

Bridgeport

Bolton

BIG BLACK RIVER
MAY 17

BRIDGE

Edward's Station

CHAMPION'S HILL
MAY 16

Jackson
MAY 14

CANAL

Warrenton

BIG BLACK RIVER

Raymond

MAY 12

New Carthage

MISSISSIPPI RIVER

BIG

PEARL RIVER

Rocky Springs

Hard Times

Grand Gulf

BAYOU

PIERRE

De Shroon's

Port Gibson

Bruinsburg

MAY 1

Miles
0 2 4 6 8

Route of Grant's Army from Milliken's Bend to Vicksburg April-May 1863

Cliff Young

Stanton's Observer
at Vicksburg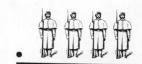

The major Union objective in the West was the reopening of the Mississippi, which would cut the Confederacy in two. Vicksburg was the principal Confederate stronghold on the river. For many months Grant tried to approach the citadel, overland and by water. All efforts seemed in vain, and in the North criticism mounted. In the spring of 1863, Secretary of War Edwin M. Stanton sent Charles A. Dana to Grant's headquarters, ostensibly to investigate the pay service but actually to observe and report daily in cipher on operations in the Western command. Dana stayed with Grant until the siege was over and the most daring of that general's campaigns had been won with the surrender of the Confederate fortress on July 4. Dana came to know the general well.

As soon as I arrived at Milliken's Bend, on April 6th, I had hunted up Grant and explained my mission. He received me cordially. Indeed, I think Grant was always glad to have me with his army. He did not like letter writing, and my daily dispatches to Mr. Stanton relieved him from the necessity of describing every day what was going on in the army. From the first neither he nor any of his staff or corps commanders evinced any unwillingness to show me the inside of things. In this first interview at Milliken's Bend, for instance, Grant explained to me fully his new plan of campaign— for there was now but one—that by three o'clock I was able to send an outline of it to Mr. Stanton. From that time I saw and knew all the interior operations of that toughest of tough jobs, the reopening of the Mississippi.

The new project, so Grant told me, was to transfer his army to New Carthage, and from there carry it over the Mississippi, landing it at or about Grand Gulf; to capture this point, and then to operate rapidly on the southern and eastern shore of the Big Black River, threatening at the same time both Vicksburg and Jackson, and confusing the Confederates as to his real objective. If this could be done he believed the enemy would come out of Vicksburg and fight.

The first element in this plan was to open a passage from the Mississippi near Milliken's Bend, above Vicksburg, to the bayou on the west side, which led around to New Carthage below. The length of navigation in this cut-off was about thirty-seven miles and the plan was to take through with small tugs perhaps fifty barges, enough, at least, to transfer the whole army, with artillery and horses, to the other side of the Mississippi in twenty-four hours. If necessary, troops were to be transported by the canal though Grant hoped to march them by the road along its bank. Part of McClernand's Corps had already reached New Carthage overland, and Grant was hurrying other troops forward. The canal in the bayou was already half completed, thirty-five hundred men being at work on it when I arrived.

The second part of the plan was to float down the river past the Vicksburg batteries, half a dozen steamboats protected by defenses of bales of cotton and wet hay; these steamboats were to serve as transports of supplies after the army had crossed the Mississippi.

Perhaps the best evidence of the feasibility of the project was found in the fact that the river men pronounced its success certain. General Sherman, who commanded one of the three corps in Grant's army, and with whom I conversed at length upon the subject, thought there was no difficulty in opening the passage, but that the line would be a precarious one for supplies after the army was

Running the Confederate Batteries at Vicksburg. *From a painting by J. E. Taylor, June 1883, belonging to Admiral David D. Porter. Collections of the Library of Congress.*

thrown across the Mississippi. Sherman's preference was for a movement by way of Yazoo Pass, or Lake Providence, but it was not long before I saw in our daily talks that his mind was tending to the conclusion of General Grant. As for General Grant, his purpose was dead set on the new scheme. Admiral Porter cordially agreed with him.

Living at headquarters as I did throughout the siege of Vicksburg, I soon became intimate with General Grant, not only knowing every operation while it was still but an idea, but studying its execution on the spot. Grant was an uncommon fellow—the most modest, the most disinterested, and the most honest man I ever knew, with a temper that nothing could disturb, and a judgment that was judicial in its comprehensiveness and wisdom. Not a great man, except morally; not an original or brilliant man, but sincere, thoughtful, deep, and gifted with courage that never faltered; when the time came to risk all, he went in like a simple-hearted, unaffected, unpretending hero, whom no ill omens could deject and no triumph unduly exalt. A social, friendly man, too, fond of a pleasant joke and also ready with one; but liking above all a long chat of an evening, and ready to sit up with you all night, talking in the cool breeze in front of his tent. Not a man of sentimentality, not demonstrative in friendship, but always holding to his friends, and just even to the enemies he hated.

Charles A. Dana, *Recollections of the Civil War.*

"A Grateful Acknowledgment"

The capture of Vicksburg and its large garrison, with the Union control of the Mississippi that followed, was one of the decisive events of the Civil War. In the North it was somewhat overshadowed by the great battle of Gettysburg, where the terrifying Confederate invasion of Pennsylvania under General Robert E. Lee had been turned back. But the President, who was rapidly becoming a shrewd judge of military operations, knew and recognized Grant's achievement for what it was. His faith in this much-abused general had been justified and the letter of appreciation that he promptly wrote Grant was heart-warming.

Executive Mansion,
Washington, July 13, 1863.

Major General Grant
   My dear General
      I do not remember that you and I ever met personally. I write this now as a grateful acknowledgment for the almost inestimable service you have done the country. I wish to say a word further. When you first reached the vicinity of Vicksburg, I thought you should do, what you finally did—march the troops across the neck, run the batteries with the transports, and thus go below; and I never had any faith, except a general hope that you knew better than I, that the Yazoo Pass expedition, and the like, could succeed. When you got below, and took Port-Gibson, Grand Gulf, and vicin-

President Lincoln thanks General Grant for the Vicksburg victory. *Reproduced with the permission of the Historical Society of Pennsylvania, Philadelphia.*

ity, I thought you should go down the river and join Gen. Banks; and when you turned Northward East of the Big Black, I feared it was a mistake. I now wish to make the personal acknowledgment that you were right, and I was wrong.

Yours very truly
A. Lincoln

The Collected Works of Abraham Lincoln

A Desperate Situation

After the fall of Vicksburg, Grant's powerful army was scattered by the higher command, instead of being used in an operation against Mobile as he proposed. The critical action in the West shifted to eastern Tennessee. In the autumn Grant was called to redeem a desperate situation there, where the Confederate forces under General Braxton Bragg were besieging the Union army under General William Rosecrans in Chattanooga. Grant recalled graphically in the Memoirs what he found on his arrival.

osecrans had very skillfully manoeuvred Bragg south of the Tennessee River, and through and beyond Chattanooga. If he had stopped and intrenched, and made himself strong there, all would have been right and the mistake of not moving earlier partially compensated. But he pushed on, with his forces very much scattered, until Bragg's troops from Mississippi began to join him. Then Bragg took the initiative. Rosecrans had to fall back in turn, and was able to get his army together at Chickamauga, some miles south-east of Chattanooga, before the main battle was brought on. The battle was fought on the 19th and 20th of September, and Rosecrans was badly defeated, with a heavy loss in artillery and some sixteen thousand men killed, wounded and captured. The corps under Major-General George H. Thomas stood its ground, while Rosecrans, with Crittenden and McCook, returned to Chattanooga. Thomas returned also, but later, and with his troops in good order. Bragg followed and took possession of Missionary Ridge, overlooking Chattanooga. He also occupied Lookout Mountain, west of the town, which Rosecrans had abandoned, and with it his control of the river and the river road as far back as Bridgeport. The National troops were now strongly intrenched in Chattanooga Valley, with the Tennessee River behind them and the enemy occupying commanding heights to the east and west, with a strong line across the valley from mountain to mountain, and with Chattanooga Creek, for a large part of the way, in front of their line.

On the 29th Halleck telegraphed me the above results, and directed all the forces that could be spared from my department to be sent to Rosecrans. Long before this dispatch was received Sherman was on his way, and McPherson was moving east with most of the garrison of Vicksburg.

A retreat at that time would have been a terrible disaster. It would not only have been the loss of a most important strategic position to us, but it would have been attended with the loss of all the artillery still left with the Army of the Cumberland and the annihilation of that army itself, either by capture or demoralization.

All supplies for Rosecrans had to be brought from Nashville. The railroad between this base and the army was in possession of the government to Bridgeport, the point at which the road crosses to the south side of the Tennessee River; but Bragg, holding Lookout and Raccoon mountains west of Chattanooga, commanded the railroad, the river and the shortest and best wagon-roads, both south and north of the Tennessee, between Chattanooga and Bridgeport. The distance between these two places is but twenty-six miles by rail; but owing to the position of Bragg, all supplies for Rosecrans had to be hauled by a circuitous route north of the river over a mountainous country, increasing the distance to over sixty miles.

The country afforded but little food for his animals, nearly ten thousand of which had already starved, and not enough were left to draw a single piece of artillery or even the ambulances to convey the sick. The men had been on half rations of hard bread for a considerable time, with but few other supplies except beef driven from Nashville across the country. The region along the road became so

The battle at Chickamauga.

exhausted of food for the cattle that by the time they reached Chattanooga they were much in the condition of the few animals left alive there—"on the lift." Indeed, the beef was so poor that the soldiers were in the habit of saying, with a faint facetiousness, that they were living on "half rations of hard bread and *beef dried on the hoof.*"

Nothing could be transported but food, and the troops were without sufficient shoes or other clothing suitable for the advancing season. What they had was well worn. The fuel within the Federal lines was exhausted, even to the stumps of trees. There were no teams to draw it from the opposite bank, where it was abundant. The only way of supplying fuel, for some time before my arrival, had been to cut trees on the north bank of the river at a considerable distance up the stream, form rafts of it and float it down with the current, effecting a landing on the south side within our lines by the use of paddles or poles. It would then be carried on the shoulders of the men to their camps.

If a retreat had occurred at this time it is not probable that any of the army would have reached the railroad as an organized body, if followed by the enemy.

Personal Memoirs of U. S. Grant.

51

Meeting the New Chief

Grant's new command, the Military Division of the Mississippi, included all the territory between the river and the mountains. His first act was to replace Rosecrans with Thomas in command of the Army of the Cumberland, now under siege in Chattanooga. Thomas promised by wire to hold the town until he starved. Late in October the new chief arrived. Horace Porter, a young ordnance officer, now met the man he was to serve and know long and intimately.

While sitting in my quarters in the little town of Chattanooga, Tennessee, about an hour after nightfall, Friday, October 23, 1863, an orderly brought me a message from General George H. Thomas, Commander of the Army of the Cumberland, on whose staff I was serving, summoning me to headquarters. A storm had been raging for two days, and a chilling rain was still falling. A few minutes' walk brought me to the plain wooden, one-story dwelling occupied by the commander, which was situated on Walnut street, near Fourth, and upon my arrival I found him in the front room on the left side of the hall, with three members of his staff and several strange officers. In an arm-chair facing the fireplace was seated a general officer, slight in figure and of medium stature, whose face bore an expression of weariness. He was carelessly dressed, and his uniform coat was unbuttoned and thrown back from his chest. He held a lighted cigar in his mouth, and sat in a stooping posture, with his head bent slightly forward. His clothes were wet, and his trousers and top-boots were spattered with mud. General Thomas approached this officer, and, turning to me and mentioning me by name, said, "I want to present you to General Grant." Thereupon the officer seated in the chair, without changing his position, glanced up, extended his arm to its full length, shook hands, and said in a low voice, and speaking slowly, "How do you do?" This was my first meeting with the man with whom I was destined afterward to spend so many of the most interesting years of my life.

General Grant had started, the day before the incident I have described, for Bridgeport, a place thirty miles below Chattanooga, where the Nashville and Chattanooga Railroad crosses the Tennessee River, and had ridden by way of Walden's Ridge, the only route left open by which communication could be had with the beleaguered town. We had been advised that he was on his way, but hardly expected that he would reach Chattanooga that night, considering the state of the weather, the wretched condition of the roads, or rather bridle-paths, over the mountain, and the severe injury to his leg which had been caused by a fall of his horse several weeks before, and from which he was still suffering. When he arrived he had to be lifted from his saddle, and was evidently experiencing much pain, as his horse had slipped in coming down the mountain, and had further injured the lame leg; but the general showed less signs of fatigue than might have been supposed after his hard ride of two days under such trying circumstances.

As soon as General Grant had partaken of a light supper immediately after his arrival, General Thomas had sent for several general officers and most of the members of his staff to come to headquarters, and the room soon contained an exceedingly interesting group. A member of General Thomas's staff quietly called that officer's attention to the fact that the distinguished guest's clothes were pretty wet and his boots were thoroughly soaked with rain after his long ride through the storm, and intimated that colds were usually no respecters of persons. General Thomas's mind had been so intent upon receiving the commander, and arranging for a conference of officers, that he had entirely overlooked his guest's travel-stained condition; but as soon as his attention was called to it, all of his old-time Virginia hospitality was aroused, and he at once begged his newly arrived chief to step into a bedroom and change his clothes. His urgings, however, were in vain. The general thanked him politely, but positively declined to make any additions to his personal comfort, except to light a fresh cigar. Afterward, however, he consented to draw his chair nearer to the wood fire which was burning in the chimney-place, and to thrust his feet forward to give his top-boots a chance to dry. The extent of his indulgence in personal comfort in the field did not seem to be much greater than that of bluff old Marshal Suvaroff, who, when he wished to give himself over to an excess of luxury, used to go so far as to take off one spur before going to bed.

At General Grant's request, General Thomas, General William F. Smith, his chief engineer, commonly known in the army as "Baldy" Smith, and others, pointed out on a large map the various positions of the troops, and described the general situation. General Grant sat for some time as immovable as a rock and as silent as the sphinx, but listened attentively to all that was said. After a while he straightened himself up in his chair, his features assumed an air of animation, and in a tone of voice which manifested a deep interest in the discussion, he began to fire whole volleys of questions at the officers present. So intelligent were his inquiries, and so pertinent his suggestions, that he made a profound impression upon every one by the quickness of his perception and the knowledge which he had already acquired regarding important details of the army's condition. His questions showed from the outset that his mind was dwelling not only upon the prompt opening of a line of supplies, but upon taking the offensive against the enemy. In this he was only manifesting one of his chief military characteristics—an inborn dislike to be thrown upon the defensive. Even when he had to defend a position, his method of warfare was always that of the "offensive-defensive."

Horace Porter, *Campaigning with Grant.*

The Heights of Fame

The offensive operations that Grant planned to break the siege at Chattanooga were carried out successfully, though not entirely according to the plan, late in November. The dramatic three-days' battle was a great Union victory, but the decisive assault on Missionary Ridge was pushed through without orders by the soldiers themselves, eager to avenge their defeat at Chickamauga. Nevertheless, this time Grant received full credit for the victory and his fame resounded to the skies. That winter the Congress passed an act

reviving the rank of lieutenant general, carrying with it the command of the armies of the Union, and Lincoln named Grant for the place. In this rise to the military heights, Grant did not forget the subordinates who had served him long and ably. Generals William Tecumseh Sherman and James B. McPherson had been with him since Shiloh. To them he felt especially grateful.

Nashville, Tennessee,
March 4th 1864.

Dear Sherman,

The bill reviving the grade of Lieut. Gen. in the Army has become a law and my name has been sent to the Senate for the place. I now receive orders to report to Washington in person, immediately, which indicates either a confirmation or a likelihood of confirmation. I start in the morning to comply with the order but I shall say very distinctly on my arrival there that I accept no appointment which will require me to make that City my Hd Qrs. This however is not what I started out to write about.

Whilst I have been eminently successful in this War, in at least gaining the confidence of the public, no one feels more than me how much of this success is due to the energy, skill, and harmonious puting forth of that energy and skill, of those who it has been my good fortune to have occupying a subordinate position under me. There are many officers to whom these remarks are applicable to a greater or less degree, proportionate to their ability as soldiers, but what I want is to express my thanks to you and McPherson as *the men* to whom, above all others, I feel indebted for whatever I have had of success. How far your execution of whatever has been given you to do entitles you to the reward I am receiving you cannot know as well as me. I feel all the gratitude this letter would express, giving it the most flattering construction.

The word *You* I use in the plural intending it for Mc. also. I should write to him, and will some day, but starting in the morning I do not know that I will find time just now.

Your friend

U. S. Grant
Maj. Gen.

U. S. Grant Papers, Library of Congress.

Planning the Final Campaign

Grant found that his headquarters must be in the East, with the Army of the Potomac, where he could direct in person the operations against Lee's formidable Army of Northern Virginia. He designated Sherman to take over his former command in the Mississippi Valley, opposed to the Confederate Army of Tennessee under General Joseph E. Johnston. The Union armies East and West had never been properly coordinated nor used so aggressively as to bring their superior strength fully and steadily to bear upon the enemy. It was Grant's purpose to remedy this. What had been "a balky team," as he described it, was to be made to pull together in harness. Before the campaign of 1864 opened, he returned to the West for a last conference with Sherman. Sherman told about it many years later at a meeting of Union veterans, gathered together in the Burnet House in Cincinnati to fight their battles over again.

Right here, in this very house, yonder in the room within the sound of my voice, began the campaign for Atlanta. General Grant sent to me when I was on the Mississippi to be at Nashville on a certain day, but we found ourselves so overwhelmed with details that we concluded to postpone any immediate conference, such as ought to precede all grand events, until we had leisure time on the way from Nashville to Cincinnati. In the cars we could speak but little for the rattle and jarring, but when we got to this hotel, the old Burnet House, we were at rest, and for hours we looked over these maps in yonder room, which seems to be the reading room now, in front of the office towards Third street. . . .

In yonder room we two met, no better and no worse than our other fellow-citizens, went over the maps before us, and the long list of brigades, divisions and corps; their stations, points and quantity of tools; quantity of this thing and that thing; scattered from Knoxville clear down to Natchez on the river, out of which we were to form an army to go to Atlanta, not for Atlanta, but because we judged that that was the route on which they were to retreat, and on which we made up our minds they *should* retreat.

General Grant, magnanimous as ever, concluded to go East; a stranger almost among strange troops, volunteers; a more daring thing was never done by man on earth. But he went there, and studied the little idiosyncracies of the different armies there, and we finally settled down upon a plan. He was to go for Lee, and Sherman was to go for Joe Johnston. That was his plan.

Report of the Proceedings of the Society
of the Army of the Tennessee, 1889.

Lieutenant General Grant—1864. *Collections of the Library of Congress.*

The New Man
From the West

There were other generals and other armies in the field, but what happened between Grant and Lee, and between Sherman and Johnston, was to decide the issue. Sherman knew his men and they knew and trusted him, but Grant was a stranger to the Army of the Potomac. That army had seen many generals come and go. A staff officer in General John Sedgwick's Sixth Corps tells of the impression the new commander made.

As spring approached, the army daily became larger from fresh enlistments and the return of those who had been wounded or exchanged from prison. Rumor told us that General Grant was coming to take command. As we had sad experience of a Western general with his headquarters in the saddle, we were half inclined not to like it much; but the record and Lincoln's opinion were in his favor, and when it became understood that he was to have his own way without interference from Washington, we determined to let our opinions of him be governed by the events to come. While never very enthusiastic over Grant, the Army of the Potomac forgave the cruel and unnecessary losses they sustained under him on account of the results attained. It was not that enthusiasm had died out among us, for Sheridan could rouse plenty of it afterward, but we had exhausted much of our early fervor, and envied the Confederates their great captain.

Then too, we thought people North hardly comprehended that the Army of the Potomac had been fighting the choicest leadership and the best army by far of the Confederacy, and all the time with a rope around its neck tied to the doors of the war department. But Grant came, and brought the little fellow with him named Sheridan to command the cavalry, and we began to think that perhaps they would do the business after all. They reviewed us, corps after corps, and emulation as to who would make the best appearance ran high. General Torbert of the New Jersey brigade was a very handsome man and the best-dressed officer in the army. He had magnificent horses, a saddle which was said to have cost five hundred dollars, with acoutrements to match, and when he passed a reviewing stand it usually caused a sensation. As our corps passed General Grant, from our proper places, we watched him carefully for some expression or mark of approval, but so far as we could see he did not seem even to be thinking.

After we got back to camp and had dismounted, Whittier asked, "What did General Grant think of us? What did he say, General? He made one remark to you." "He said Torbert rode a good horse," replied the general, as he sought the interior of his tent and his everlasting game of "solitaire." We would like to know the exact words of Napoleon or Wellington on any occasion, and posterity may want to know likewise the words of Grant, the taciturn, and it is certain that to others than his very intimates they were few in number.

Thomas W. Hyde, *Following the Greek Cross: Or, Memories of the Sixth Army Corps.*

"May God Sustain You"

As the time drew near when all the armies of the Union were to advance simultaneously in a concerted effort to bring the Confed-

eracy to its knees, Lincoln wrote once more to Grant, speeding him to the battle.

Executive Mansion
Washington, April 30, 1864

Lieutenant General Grant,

Not expecting to see you again before the Spring campaign opens, I wish to express, in this way, my entire satisfaction with what you have done up to this time, so far as I understand it. The particulars of your plans I neither know, or seek to know. You are vigilant and self-reliant; and, pleased with this, I wish not to obtrude any constraints or restraints upon you. While I am very anxious that any great disaster, or the capture of our men in great numbers, shall be avoided, I know these points are less likely to escape your attention than they would be mine — If there is anything wanting which is within my power to give, do not fail to let me know it.

And now with a brave Army, and a just cause, may God sustain you.

Yours very truly

A. Lincoln

The Collected Works of Abraham Lincoln

Grant was grateful to Lincoln for this expression of confidence, and for the whole-hearted support that the President had given him. He hastened to say so.

Headquarters, Armies of the United States,
Culpeper Court House, Virginia, May 1, 1864

The President: Your very kind letter of yesterday is just received. The confidence you express for the future and satisfaction for the past in my military administration is acknowledged with pride. It shall be my earnest endeavor that you and the country shall not be disappointed. From my first entrance into the volunteer service of the country to the present day, I have never had cause of complaint —have never expressed or implied a complaint against the Administration or the Secretary of War, for throwing any embarrassment in the way of my vigorously prosecuting what appeared to be my duty. And since the promotion which placed me in command of all the armies, and in view of the great responsibility and the importance of success, I have been astonished at the readiness with which everything asked for has been yielded, without even an explanation being asked. Should my success be less than I desire and expect, the least I can say is, the fault is not with you.

Very truly, your obedient servant,
U. S. Grant, Lieutenant-General

Battles and Leaders of the Civil War.

South After the Wilderness

Early in May Grant crossed the Rapidan, which had all winter separated the opposing armies in Virginia. Lee moved at once to strike him and there followed two days of desperate fighting in the tangled thickets of the Wilderness. An officer of the 16th Maine, in the Fifth Corps of the Army of the Potomac, after recording the first day's fight as he saw it, has told what came after. The outcome of the battle of the Wilderness presented a test of Grant's will. Both armies sensed it.

We manned our works all night in the edge of the woods. There was no moon to light the clearing, only dim stars, and the air was hazy and pungent with the smoke and smell of fires yet smouldering. We couldn't see the wounded and dying, whose cries

Grant's first test in the East—the battle in the Wilderness.

we heard all too clearly; nor could our stretcher bearers go out to find them and bring them in; the opposing lines were near, and the rebels were fidgety and quick to shoot.

At daybreak we were relieved and sent to the rear to make coffee and breakfast. Colonel Leonard then being absent, sick, Colonel Lyle was assigned to the command of the brigade. We were moved back nearly to our old position. Ahead of us throughout the morning there was fighting, but we were not engaged. Early in the afternoon the brigade was withdrawn, moved to the left, and placed in reserve with some heavy artillery troops near the Orange Court House plank road. Later there was fierce fighting near by, but again we were not engaged. We threw up breastworks under skirmish fire, and stayed behind them that night.

Saturday, May 7th, we stood in expectation of more fighting, and strengthened our works; but the battle was over. Neither side had driven the other. Rumors came that Lee was retreating. We doubted that. What would Grant do? By evening we had our answer; the right of the Union line moved in rear of the left. We heard on the still evening air a sound of distant cheering from the rebels. Had they seen the move? Did they suppose that Grant was falling back? Our division was massed not far from Wilderness Church, and from there, we knew, the turnpike led to Chancellorsville. Would Grant, like Hooker, draw back, and then retreat to the north side of the Rappahannock? No. When we started, at eight o'clock that night, we headed south. Our men knew what that meant. Somewhere, Grant was seen, and a great burst of cheering greeted him as he rode swiftly and silently by.

Abner R. Small, *The Road to Richmond.*

Grant moves south from the Wilderness.

"Fight it Out on This Line"

Leaving the Wilderness, Grant sought to pass Lee's right by Spotsylvania Court House. Lee was there before him and another grim conflict quickly shaped up. Elihu B. Washburne, congressman from the Galena district in Illinois, had sponsored Grant's appointment to a brigadier generalship in 1861 and had defended him in his time of trouble later. Washburne spent the first few days of the Virginia campaign as Grant's guest at headquarters.

The 11th of May gave promise of a little rest for everybody, as the commander expressed his intention to spend the day simply in reconnoitering for the purpose of learning more about the character and strength of the enemy's intrenchments, and discovering the weakest points in his line, with a view to breaking through. He sat down at the mess-table that morning, and made his entire breakfast off a cup of coffee and a small piece of beef cooked almost to a crisp; for the cook had by this time learned that the nearer he came to burning up the beef the better the general liked it. During the short time he was at the table he conversed with Mr. Elihu B. Washburne, who had accompanied headquarters up to this time, and who was now about to return to Washington. After breakfast the general lighted a cigar, seated himself on a camp-chair in front of his tent, and was joined there by Mr. Washburne and several members of the staff. At half-past eight o'clock the cavalry escort which was to accompany the congressman was drawn up in the road near by, and all present rose to bid him good-by. Turning to the chief, he said: "General, I shall go to see the President and the Secretary of War as soon as I reach Washington. I can imagine their anxiety to know what you think of the prospects of the campaign, and I know they would be greatly gratified if I could carry a message from you giving what encouragement you can as to the situation."

The general hesitated a moment, and then replied: "We are certainly making fair progress, and all the fighting has been in our favor; but the campaign promises to be a long one, and I am particularly anxious not to say anything just now that might hold out false hopes to the people"; and then, after a pause, added, "However, I will write a letter to Halleck, as I generally communicate through him, giving the general situation, and you can take it with you." He stepped into his tent, sat down at his field-table, and, keeping his cigar in his mouth, wrote a despatch of about two hundred words. In the middle of the communication occurred the famous words, "I propose to fight it out on this line if it takes all summer." When the letter had been copied, he folded it and handed it to Mr. Washburne, who thanked him warmly, wished him a continuation of success, shook hands with him and with each of the members of the staff, and at once mounted his horse and rode off. The staff-officers read the retained copy of the despatch, but neither the general himself nor any one at headquarters realized the epigrammatic character of the striking sentence it contained until the New York papers reached camp a few days afterward with the words displayed in large headlines, and with conspicuous comments upon the force of the expression. It was learned afterward that the President was delighted to read this despatch giving such full information as to the situation, and that he had said a few days before, when asked by a member of Congress what Grant was doing: "Well, I can't tell much about it. You see, Grant has gone to the Wilderness, crawled in, drawn up the ladder, and pulled in the hole after him, and I guess we'll have to wait till he comes out before we know just what he's up to."

Horace Porter, *Campaigning with Grant.*

"A Scientific Goth"

All through the rest of May and well into June, the armies were in daily contact. Skirmishing was almost constant, alternating with heavy assault and counter-attack. Grant maneuvered steadily by his left between battles, toward Richmond and the James. Lee met every move, pushing to his right and time and again presenting an unbreakable front. The world had never seen such a relentless campaign on so grand a scale. Shortly after the battle of Cold Harbor, though Grant met there a bloody check, an imaginative staff officer of Lee's foresaw the end.

The struggle for the Salient at Spotsylvania Court House.

Headquarters of General Robert E. Lee,
Near Mechanicsville, Hanover County, Va., June 7, 1864.

Maj. Gen. Sterling Price,
 Commanding District of Arkansas:

My Dear General: Since active operations commenced on the Rapidan and the enemy crossed over, I have been riding with the staff of General Lee, and so passed through the battles of the Wilderness, of Spotsylvania Court House, and of those since fought here on the line of the Chickahominy. Up to this time our loss in killed, wounded, and prisoners does not exceed 18,000, while that of the enemy in similar respects is not less than 70,000. But both armies have been built up through re-enforcements to their original standard, and other battles have still to be fought equally bloody with the bloodiest. Here on the Chickahominy we occupy Mc-Clellan's old line, with this difference, we face to the east, whereas he faced to the west; hence Jackson's attack upon him was in his rear, whereas Grant's attack on us is to our front. From first to last Grant has shown great skill and prudence combined with remorseless persistency and brutality. He is a scientific Goth resembling Alaric, destroying the country as he goes, and delivering the people over to starvation. Nor does he bury his dead, but leaves them to rot on the battle-field. He has commenced again sliding his right down past his left, doubtless in order to reach Bottom's Bridge and the Long Bridge with the intention of crossing to the Richmond side. Lee, accordingly, is throwing down his left. On both sides I apprehend the lines will be contracted and massed, and a desperate encounter take place in the course of the movement. In view of the fact, just arrived by telegraph, that the enemy in the Valley have defeated and killed General Jones and taken Staunton, and now have the Valley at their mercy—the remainder of our troops having been drawn here under Breckenridge from that quarter—it may be, and probably is, Grant's design to make across the James River to seize our communications, and thus to assure the destruction of our supplies and compel a surrender ultimately through starvation. Should he succeed in getting over the James and in forming his lines across our railroads on the south side, our situation will be at least uncomfortable, if not alarming, and I am unable to see, without the intervention of some special Providence, any assurance of a successful termination of the war on our part this year or the next. But Providence and a good cause may save us here as they seem to have saved you all in the Texas-Mississippi; in despite of bad management and against every human calculation.

Grant's Army Crossing the James River.
From Horace Porter, Campaigning with Grant *(The Century Co., New York, 1897).*

The game going on upon the military chess board between Lee and Grant has been striking and grand, surpassing anything I have heretofore witnessed, and conducted on both sides with consummate mastery of the art of war. It is admitted that Lee has at last met with a foeman who watches (matches) his steel, although he may not be worthy of it. Each guards himself perfectly and gives his blow, with a precise eye and cool and sanguinary nerve. . . .

John Tyler,
C. S. Army

Official Records of the Union and Confederate Armies.

The Crossing of the James

With Lee's lines closely drawn about Richmond, opposing Grant on much the same ground where McClellan's army had been driven back two years before, Grant suddenly broke the pattern of maneuver, withdrew from Lee's front and threw his army across the James. His new objective was Petersburg, through which passed Lee's supplies from the Carolinas.

The work of laying the great pontoon bridge across the James began after 4 p.m. on June 14, and was finished by eleven o'clock that night. It was twenty-one hundred feet in length, and required one hundred and one pontoons. The pontoons, which were in the channel of the river, where the water was swift and deep, were attached to vessels that were anchored above and below for this purpose. . . .

By midnight of the 16th the army, with all its artillery and trains had been safely transferred to the south side of the James, without a serious accident or the loss of a wagon or an animal, and with no casualties except those which occurred in the minor encounters of Warren's corps and the cavalry with the enemy. This memorable operation, when examined in all its details, will furnish one of the most valuable and instructive studies in logistics.

As the general-in-chief stood upon the bluff on the north bank of the river on the morning of June 15, watching with unusual interest the busy scene spread out before him, it presented a sight which had never been equaled even in his extended experience in all the varied phases of warfare. His cigar had been thrown aside, his hands were clasped behind him, and he seemed lost in the contemplation of the spectacle. The great bridge was the scene of a continuous movement of infantry columns, batteries of artillery, and wagon-trains. The approaches to the river on both banks were covered with masses of troops moving briskly to their positions or waiting patiently their turn to cross. At the two improvised ferries, steamboats were gliding back and forth with the regularity of weavers' shuttles. A fleet of transports covered the surface of the water below the bridge, and gunboats floated lazily upon the stream, guarding the river above. Drums were beating the march, bands were playing stirring quicksteps, the distant booming of cannon on Warren's front showed that he and the enemy were still exchanging compliments; and mingled with these sounds were the cheers of the sailors, the shouting of the troops, the rumbling of wheels, and the shrieks of steam-whistles. The bright sun, shining through a clear sky upon the scene, cast its sheen upon the water, was reflected from the burnished gun-barrels and glittering cannon, and brought out with increased brilliancy the gay colors of the waving banners. The calmly flowing river reflected the blue of the heavens, and mirrowed on its surface the beauties of nature that bordered it. The rich grain was standing high in the surrounding fields. The harvest was almost ripe, but the harvesters had fled. The arts of civilization had recoiled before the science of destruction; and in looking from the growing crops to the marching columns, the gentle smile of peace contrasted strangely with the savage frown of war. It was a matchless pageant that could not fail to inspire all beholders with the grandeur of achievement and the majesty of military power. The man whose genius had conceived and whose skill had executed this masterly movement stood watching the spectacle in profound silence. Whether his mind was occupied with the contemplation of its magnitude and success, or was busied with maturing plans for the future, no one can tell. After a time he woke from his reverie, mounted his horse, and gave orders to have headquarters ferried across to the south bank of the river. . . .

Horace Porter, *Campaigning with Grant.*

The Indulgent Father

Petersburg was scantily garrisoned and Grant's rapid maneuver almost succeeded. But before the Union corps commanders on the ground pushed home their assault, reinforcements from Lee's army arrived. The assault was beaten off and the armies settled down to siege operations. More than once in the Western campaigns, Grant had brought Julia and some of the children to camp with him. The close and deadly fighting from the Wilderness to Cold Harbor and beyond had not permitted him this luxury, but after the Petersburg front had become more or less stabilized he sent for his family to pay him a visit. While they were at City Point, a member of the staff caught the general in a very undignified position.

Mrs. Grant had come East with the children, and Colonel Dent, her brother, was sent to meet them at Philadelphia, and bring them to City Point to pay a visit to the general. The children con-

General and Mrs. Grant and son Jesse at City Point, Va., 1865. *Collections of the Library of Congress.*

sisted of Frederick D., then fourteen years old; Ulysses S., Jr., twelve; Nellie R., nine; and Jesse R., six. Nellie was born on the 4th of July, and when a child an innocent deception had been practiced upon her by her father in letting her believe that all the boisterous demonstrations and display of fireworks on Independence day were in honor of her birthday. The general was exceedingly fond of his family, and his meeting with them afforded him the happiest day he had seen since they parted. They were comfortably lodged aboard the headquarters steamboat, but spent most of their time in camp. The morning after their arrival, when I stepped into the general's tent, I found him in his shirt-sleeves engaged in a rough-and-tumble wrestling-match with the two older boys. He had become red in the face, and seemed nearly out of breath from the exertion. The lads had just tripped him up, and he was on his knees on the floor grappling with the youngsters, and joining in their merry laughter, as if he were a boy again himself. I had several despatches in my hand, and when he saw that I had come on business, he disentangled himself after some difficulty from the young combatants, rose to his feet, brushed the dust off his knees with his hand, and said in a sort of apologetic manner: "Ah, you know my weaknesses—my children and my horses." The children often romped with him, and he joined in their frolics as if they were all playmates together. The younger ones would hang about his neck while he was writing, make a terrible mess of his papers, and turn everything in his tent into a toy: but they were never once reproved for any innocent sport; they were governed solely by an appeal to their affections. They were always respectful, and never failed to render strict obedience to their father when he told them seriously what he wanted them to do.

Horace Porter, *Campaigning with Grant.*

Sherman's Estimate of Grant

Though Grant tried during the summer and autumn to extend his lines to the left around Petersburg, so as to cut Lee's rail communications, his efforts met with only limited success. Meanwhile, in the West, Sherman had driven down through northern Georgia and had finally taken Atlanta. In the Confederate army opposing him, General John B. Hood had replaced Johnston. After giving up Atlanta, Hood moved to cut Sherman's line of communications back to Chattanooga. Sherman went in pursuit. While he was operating against Hood, Grant sent to him General James H. Wilson to reorganize his cavalry. Wilson reported to Sherman late in October at Gaylesville, Alabama.

During the memorable night at Gaylesville Sherman asked many questions about Grant, the condition of his army, and the progress he was making toward finishing the great work before him in Virginia. He commented freely on Grant's delays and disappointments, and while he acknowledged the importance of Sheridan's victories in the Valley, he felt that the deadlock in south Virginia would last till his own army could reenforce Grant's in front of Petersburg. He also commented freely on the strong as well as the weak points of Grant's character and in the midst of the conversation looked up suddenly, with the glow of the camp fire on his deeply marked features and exclaimed: "Wilson, I am a damned sight smarter man than Grant: I know a great deal more about war, military history, strategy, and grand tactics than he does; I know more about organization, supply, and administration and about everything else than he does; but I'll tell you where he beats me and where he beats the world. He don't care a damn for what the enemy does out of his sight, but it scares me like hell." He added: "I am more nervous than he is. I am more likely to change my orders or to countermarch my command than he is. He uses such information as he has according to his best judgment; he issues his orders and does his level best to carry them out without much reference to what is going on about him and, so far, experience seems to have fully justified him."

James H. Wilson, *Under the Old Flag.*

General Grant at City Point, Va., in 1865 as the end draws near. *Courtesy, the Frederick Hill Meserve Collection, Morristown, New Jersey.*

Grant and Lee at Appomattox. *From an illustration in Horace Porter's* Campaigning with Grant *(The Century Co., New York, 1897).*

Appomattox

In the spring of 1865 the agonizing struggle at last came to an end. Sherman's army had driven its way to the sea and northward into the Carolinas, cutting the Confederacy away from behind Lee's army. Lee abandoned Petersburg and marched westward, hoping to evade Grant and join what was left of the Confederate forces in North Carolina. Grant pursued relentlessly and, at Appomattox Court House, succeeded in planting a strong force square across Lee's path. After an exchange of letters, an armistice was arranged and the two commanders met at the house of Wilmer McLean on April 9 to discuss terms of surrender. Grant left a detailed record of this momentous meeting, as he recalled it, in his Memoirs.

Vhen I had left camp that morning I had not expected so soon the result that was then taking place, and consequently was in rough garb. I was without a sword, as I usually was when on horseback on the field, and wore a soldier's blouse for a coat, with the shoulder straps of my rank to indicate to the army who I was. When I went into the house I found General Lee. We greeted each other, and after shaking hands took our seats. I had my staff with

The price of victory.
Union cemetery at City Point, Va. U. S. Signal Corps photograph, The National Archives.

me, a good portion of whom were in the room during the whole of the interview.

What General Lee's feelings were I do not know. As he was a man of much dignity, with an impassible face, it was impossible to say whether he felt inwardly glad that the end had finally come, or felt sad over the result, and was too manly to show it. Whatever his feelings, they were entirely concealed from my observation; but my own feelings, which had been quite jubilant on the receipt of his letter, were sad and depressed. I felt like anything rather than rejoicing at the downfall of a foe who had fought so long and valiantly, and had suffered so much for a cause, though that cause was, I believe, one of the worst for which a people ever fought, and one for which there was the least excuse. I do not question, however, the sincerity of the great mass of those who were opposed to us.

General Lee was dressed in a full uniform which was entirely new, and was wearing a sword of considerable value, very likely the sword which had been presented by the State of Virginia; at all events, it was an entirely different sword from the one that would ordinarily be worn in the field. In my rough traveling suit, the uniform of a private with the straps of a lieutenant-general, I must have contrasted very strangely with a man so handsomely dressed, six feet high and of faultless form. But this was not a matter that I thought of until afterwards.

We soon fell into a conversation about old army times. He remarked that he remembered me very well in the old army; and I told him that as a matter of course I remembered him perfectly, but

The Army of Northern Virginia lays down its arms. *From a contemporary sketch by J. R. Chapin. Collections of the Library of Congress.*

from the difference in our rank and years (there being about sixteen years' difference in our ages), I had thought it very likely that I had not attracted his attention sufficiently to be remembered by him after such a long interval. Our conversation grew so pleasant that I almost forgot the object of our meeting. After the conversation had run on in this style for some time, General Lee called my attention to the object of our meeting, and said that he had asked for this interview for the purpose of getting from me the terms I proposed to give his army. I said that I meant merely that his army should lay down their arms, not to take them up again during the continuance of the war unless duly and properly exchanged. He said that he had so understood my letter.

Then we gradually fell off again into conversation about matters foreign to the subject which had brought us together. This continued for some little time, when General Lee again interrupted the course of the conversation by suggesting that the terms I proposed to give his army ought to be written out. I called to General Parker, secretary on my staff, for writing materials, and commenced writing out the following terms:

Appomattox C. H., Va.,
Apl 9th, 1865.

GEN. R. E. LEE,
Comd'g C. S. A.

GEN: In accordance with the substance of my letter to you of the 8th inst., I propose to receive the surrender of the Army of N.

Va. on the following terms, to wit: Rolls of all the officers and men to be made in duplicate. One copy to be given to an officer designated by me, the other to be retained by such officer or officers as you may designate. The officers to give their individual paroles not to take up arms against the Government of the United States until properly exchanged, and each company or regimental commander sign a like parole for the men of their commands. The arms, artillery and public property to be parked and stacked, and turned over to the officer appointed by me to receive them. This will not embrace the side-arms of the officers, nor their private horses or baggage. This done, each officer and man will be allowed to return to their homes, not to be disturbed by United States authority so long as they observe their paroles and the laws in force where they may reside.

Very respectfully,

U. S. GRANT, Lt. Gen.

When I put my pen to the paper I did not know the first word that I should make use of in writing the terms. I only knew what was in my mind, and I wished to express it clearly, so that there could be no mistaking it. As I wrote on, the thought occurred to me that the officers had their own private horses and effects, which were important to them, but of no value to us; also that it would be an unnecessary humiliation to call upon them to deliver their side arms.

No conversation, not one word, passed between General Lee and myself, either about private property, side arms, or kindred subjects. He appeared to have no objections to the terms first proposed; or if he had a point to make against them he wished to wait until they were in writing to make it. When he read over that part of the terms about side arms, horses and private property of the officers, he remarked, with some feeling, I thought, that this would have a happy effect upon his army.

Then, after a little further conversation, General Lee remarked to me again that their army was organized a little differently from the army of the United States (still maintaining by implication that we were two countries); that in their army the cavalrymen and artillerists owned their own horses; and he asked if he was to understand that the men who so owned their horses were to be permitted to retain them. I told him that as the terms were written they would not; that only the officers were permitted to take their private property. He then, after reading the terms a second time, remarked that that was clear.

I then said to him that I thought this would be about the last battle of the war—I sincerely hoped so; and I said further I took it that most of the men in the ranks were small farmers. The whole country had been so raided by the two armies that it was doubtful whether they would be able to put in a crop to carry themselves and their families through the next winter without the aid of the horses they were then riding. The United States did not want them and I would, therefore, instruct the officers I left behind to receive the paroles of his troops to let every man of the Confederate army who claimed to own a horse or mule take the animal to his home. Lee remarked again that this would have a happy effect.

He then sat down and wrote out the following letter:

Headquarters Army of Northern Virginia,
April 9, 1865.

GENERAL:—I received your letter to this date containing the terms of the surrender of the Army of Northern Virginia as proposed by you. As they are substantially the same as those expressed in your letter of the 8th inst., they are accepted. I will proceed to designate the proper officers to carry the stipulations into effect.

R. E. LEE, General.

Lieut.-General U. S. Grant.

While duplicates of the two letters were being made, the Union generals present were severally presented to General Lee.

The much talked of surrendering of Lee's sword and my handing it back, this and much more that has been said about it is the purest romance. The word sword or side arms was not mentioned by either of us until I wrote it in the terms. There was no premeditation, and it did not occur to me until the moment I wrote it down. If I had happened to omit it, and General Lee had called my attention to it, I should have put it in the terms precisely as I acceded to the provision about the soldiers retaining their horses.

General Lee, after all was completed and before taking his leave, remarked that his army was in a very bad condition for want of food, and that they were without forage; that his men had been living for some days on parched corn exclusively, and that he would have to ask me for rations and forage. I told him "certainly," and asked for how many men he wanted rations. His answer was "about twenty-five thousand:" and I authorized him to send his own commissary and quartermaster to Appomattox Station, two or three miles away, where he could have, out of the trains we had stopped, all the provisions wanted. As for forage, we had ourselves depended almost entirely upon the country for that.

Generals Gibbon, Griffin and Merritt were designated by me to carry into effect the paroling of Lee's troops before they should start for their homes—General Lee leaving Generals Longstreet, Gordon and Pendleton for them to confer with in order to facilitate this work. Lee and I then separated as cordially as we had met, he returning to his own lines, and all went into bivouac for the night at Appomattox.

The Pledged Word of U. S. Grant

The terms that Grant offered and Lee accepted promised to the Confederate soldier freedom from molestation. The assassination of President Lincoln a few days later, however, strengthened the hands of those in the Republican party who demanded vengeance. A Federal grand jury convened in Norfolk returned indictments for treason against Lee and a number of other Confederate leaders. Lee at once wrote to Grant, as one soldier to another, inquiring how this action conformed with the terms agreed upon at Appomattox. At the same time he submitted an application for a pardon under the terms of a proclamation issued by President Andrew Johnson. Grant acted promptly, sending Lee's letter to the Secretary of War with his endorsement.

Richmond 13 June '65

Genl

Upon reading the President's proclamation of the 29 ulto. I came to Richmond to ascertain what was proper or required of me to do; when I learned that with others, I was to be indicted for treason by the Grand Jury at Norfolk. I had supposed that the officers & men of the Army of N. Virga. were by the terms of their surrender protected by the U. S. Govt. from molestation, so long as they conformed to its conditions.

I am ready to meet any charges that may be preferred against me, & do not wish to avoid trial, but if I am correct as to the protection granted by my parole, & am not to be prosecuted, I desire to comply with the provisions of the President's proclamation, & therefore enclose the required application, which I request, in that event, may be acted on.

I am with great respect
your obt servt
R. E. Lee

81

Lt. Genl. U. S. Grant
Commd. the Armies of the U. States

(Endorsement)

Respectfully forwarded to the Sect of War.

In my opinion the officers and men paroled at Appomattox C. H. and since upon the same terms given to Lee, cannot be tried for treason so long as they observe the terms of their parole. This is my understanding. Good faith as well as true policy dictates that we should observe the conditions of that convention. Bad faith on the part of the Governm't or a construction of that convention subjecting officers to trial for treason, would produce a feeling of insecurity in the minds of all paroled officers and men. If so disposed they might even regard such an infraction of terms by the Government as an entire release from all obligation on their part.

I will state further that the terms granted by me met with the hearty approval of the President at the time, and of the country generally. The action of Judge Underwood in Norfolk has already had an injurious effect, and I would ask that he be ordered to quash all indictments found against paroled prisoners of war, and to desist from further prosecution of them.

U. S. Grant
Lieut. General

Hdqrs. AUS. June 16. 65

U. S. Grant Papers, Illinois State Historical Library.

While Grant's prestige at the time was enormous, this did not quite end the matter, according to his military secretary.

He went in person to discuss these papers with the President. But Andrew Johnson was not satisfied; he wanted, he said, "to make treason odious."

"When can these men be tried?" he asked.

"Never," said Grant, "unless they violate their paroles."

The President still insisted, and his Attorney-General wrote an official letter opposing Grant's contention. Finally Grant declared that he would resign his commission in the army unless the terms

Victory parade up Pennsylvania Avenue, Washington, D. C. — 1865. *Collections of the Library of Congress.*

he had granted were confirmed. I remember well the day when this occurred. He returned from the Cabinet chamber to his own headquarters and described the interview. When he recited his language he added:

"And I will keep my word. I will not stay in the army if they break the pledges that I made."

Then the resolution of the President gave way, for he found a will more stubborn, or at least more potent with the people, than his own, and orders were issued to discontinue the proceedings against Lee.

Adam Badeau, *Grant in Peace.*

One of Lee's Veterans Remembers

In accordance with the American tradition of rewarding the Nation's great military heroes, Grant was elected to the Presidency in 1868. He served two eventful terms. After leaving the White House, he spent two years in touring the world. Following his return to the United States he settled in New York City, where he lent his name to an investment firm. An unscrupulous partner brought financial ruin to Grant and many others. In an effort to pay off his debts and provide for his family, the General undertook the writing of his Memoirs. Long before the work was completed, however, he was stricken with cancer of the throat. In his desperate illness, he was cheered by tokens of respect and esteem not only from former comrades-in-arms and associates but also from former

enemies. Lee's veterans had not forgotten the generous terms ex-
tended to them at the close of the war, as one of them made clear.

Rockbridge Baths, June 30, 1885.

Genl. U. S. Grant:—

    Dr Sir:—

      I hope you will allow one who, when but a boy, laid down his arms at Appomattox and gave in his allegiance to the Union, to express his warmest sympathy for you in this your hour of affliction.

      Dear General, I have watched your movements from the hour you gave me my horse and sword and told me to go home and "assist in making a crop"—I have been proud to see the nation do you honor. And now, dear Genl in this the hour of your tribulation I weep that so brave, so magnanimous a soul must suffer as you do —
My prayer to God daily is that you dear General, may be restored to perfect health.

      And be assured that I am not the only ex-Confederate who sends his prayers daily to the throne of Grace for the restoration of the *Grandest*, the *noblest* the *bravest soldier* and the Purest Statesman who ever graced the annals of History.

      May the God who overlooked you in battle and who has brought you thus far give you grace to meet whatever He has in store for you. And may He restore you to health & friends is the fervent prayer of one who at 15 years of age entered the lists against you and accepted the magnanimous terms you accorded us at Appomattox.

I am Dear General
Yours Most Affectly

A. M. Arnold
Rockbridge Baths, Va.

U. S. Grant Papers, Illinois State Historical Library

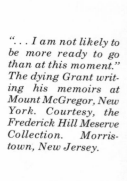

"...I am not likely to be more ready to go than at this moment." The dying Grant writing his memoirs at Mount McGregor, New York. Courtesy, the Frederick Hill Meserve Collection. Morristown, New Jersey.

The Last Battle

With the full knowledge that he was dying, Grant struggled on to complete the work that he had undertaken. In the belief that mountain air would be beneficial to him, he was moved to a cottage at Mount McGregor in the Adirondacks. There in July, 1885, he completed his personal account of his early life and his part in the Civil War, writing painfully with a pencil when he could no longer use his voice for dictation. When he had finished the manuscript, he died. A few days before the end he scribbled a note to his doctor, making it clear that it was the work on the Memoirs that had sustained him.

After all that however the disease is still there and must be fatal in the end. My life is precious of course to my family and would be to me if I could recover entirely. There never was one more willing to go than I am. I know most people have first one and then another little thing to fix up, and never get quite through. This was partially my case. I first wanted so many days to work on my book so the authorship would be clearly mine. It was graciously granted to me, after being apparently much lower than since, and with a capacity to do more work than I ever did in the same time. My work had been done so hastily that much was left out and I did all of it over from the crossing of the Rapidan River in June/64 (sic) to Appomattox. Since then I have added as much as fifty pages to the book, I should think. There is nothing more I should do to it now, and therefore I am not likely to be more ready to go than at this moment.

Horace Green, *General Grant's Last Stand.*

"Let Us Have Peace"

BIBLIOGRAPHY

BIBLIOGRAPHY

Manuscripts

Emma Dent Casey typescript, "When Grant Went a'Courtin'", Missouri Historical Society.
Grant Family Papers, Major General U. S. Grant 3rd (Ret.)
U. S. Grant Letters and Papers, Illinois State Historical Library.
U. S. Grant Papers and Letter Books, Library of Congress.
U. S. Grant Papers, Missouri Historical Society.
Elihu B. Washburne Papers, Library of Congress.

Publications

Badeau, Adam, *Grant in Peace. From Appomattox to Mount McGregor. A Personal Memoir.* S. S. Scranton & Co., Hartford, 1887.

Basler, Roy, editor, *The Collected Works of Abraham Lincoln,* 9 vols. Rutgers University Press, New Brunswick, 1953-1955.

Brinton, John H., *Personal Memoirs of John H. Brinton, Major and Surgeon U.S.V. (1861-1865).* Neale Publishing Co., New York, 1914.

Burr, Frank A., *A New, Original and Authentic Record of the Life and Deeds of General U. S. Grant.* George V. Jones, Boston, 1885.

Chetlain, Augustus L., *Recollections of Seventy Years.* Gazette Publishing Co., Galena, 1899.

Coates, Foster, "The Courtship of General Grant," *Ladies Home Journal,* October 1890.

Dana, Charles A., *Recollections of the Civil War.* D. Appleton & Co., New York, 1899.

Eaton, John and Mason, *Grant, Lincoln and the Freedmen: Reminiscences of the Civil War.* Longmans, Green & Co., New York, 1907.

Emerson, Col. John W., "Grant's Life in the West and his Mississippi Valley Campaigns," *Midland Monthly.* 1896-1898.

Grant, Ulysses S., *Personal Memoirs of U. S. Grant.* 2 vols. Charles L. Webster & Co., New York, 1885-1886.

Green, Horace, *General Grant's Last Stand: A Biography.* Charles Scribner's Sons, New York, 1936.

Hyde, Thomas W., *Following the Greek Cross: Or, Memories of the Sixth Army Corps.* Houghton, Mifflin & Co., Boston, 1894.

Johnson, R. U., and C. C. Buel, editors, *Battles and Leaders of the Civil War.* 4 vols. The Century Co., New York, 1887.

McClure, A. K., *Abraham Lincoln and Men of War-Times.* Times Publishing Co., Philadelphia, 1892.

Porter, Gen. Horace, *Campaigning with Grant.* The Century Co., New York, 1897.

Report of the Proceedings of the Society of the Army of the Tennessee—1889. Published by the Society, Cincinnati, 1893.

Small, Harold A., editor, *The Road to Richmond: the Civil War Memoirs of Major Abner R. Small, of the 16th Maine Volunteers.* University of California Press, Berkeley, 1939.

War of the Rebellion: a Compilation of the Official Record of the Union and Confederate Armies. 130 vols. Government Printing Office, Washington, 1880-1901.

Wilson, James G., *The Life and Public Services of Ulysses Simpson Grant.* DeWitt, Publisher, New York, 1885.

Wilson, James H., *Under the Old Flag.* D. Appleton & Co., New York, 1912.

ACKNOWLEDGEMENTS

The Publications Committee, Eastern National Park & Monument Association (Chairman, Rogers W. Young; Members, Benjamin H. Davis and Ralston B. Lattimore), which directed the production of this publication, and the author, wish to acknowledge, on behalf of the Association, the gracious assistance and permission given by the following individuals, organizations, and publishers:

Individuals

Gen. U. S. Grant, 3rd (Ret.), Clinton, New York, read and gave his kind approval of the text and graciously allowed us to quote excerpts from the Grant Family Papers in his possession.

Organizations

We are indebted to the following archival sources for assistance and permission to use materials from their collections: Illinois State Historical Library, Springfield; Missouri Historical Society, St. Louis; and the Manuscripts Division, Library of Congress.

Miss Virginia Daiker, Library of Congress, and Miss Josephine Cobb, The National Archives, were helpful to us in securing sketches and photographs from these institutions.

National Park Service—The staff of the Northeast Regional Office, at Philadelphia, gave us their advice, encouragement, and concurrence. Miss Lillian Cash and Mr. Joseph Cullen of the Washington Office rendered valuable assistance with many editorial details. Dr. Francis Ronalds, Superintendent, Morristown National Historical Park, Morristown, New Jersey, is due our special thanks for his good counsel and special initiative in assisting us to secure permission for the publication of one of our major sources.

We are especially grateful to Mrs. Margaret B. Klapthor, Associate Curator, Division of Political History, Smithsonian Institution, Washington, for providing the Association with a color transparency of the Cogswell portrait of General Grant and giving us permission to reproduce it.

Publishers

The Association greatly appreciates the kind permission to quote from the following published works:

Roy P. Basler, Editor, Marion Dolores Pratt and Lloyd A. Dunlap, Assistant Editors, *The Collected Works of Abraham Lincoln.* Rutgers University Press, New Brunswick, New Jersey, 1953-1955, 9 vols. Vol. VI, p. 326; Vol. VII, p. 324; permission granted by the Illinois State Historical Library, Springfield, on behalf of the Abraham Lincoln Association.

Horace Green, *General Grant's Last Stand: A Biography.* Charles Scribner's Sons, New York, 1936; permission graciously given by Mrs. Lee Gwynne Martin, New York City.

Harold A. Small, Editor, *The Road to Richmond: the Civil War Memoirs of Major Abner R. Small, of the 16th Maine Volunteers.* University of California Press, Berkeley, 1939.

55252

973.73 Pitkin